Rathad Iarainn don Gaidhealtachd

www.wayzgoose.org.uk
Tel: 01283 713674 / 821472
Copyright: Michael Pearson.
All Rights Reserved.
First Edition 2002
ISBN 0 907864 93 7

WAYZGOOSE

Printed in Italy
by STIGE
Via Pescarito 110
10099 San Mauro
Torino

Neil Gow Country - a Turbostar snakes round the curve at Inver

Getting to know the
HIGHLAND MAIN LINE

I first travelled on the Highland Main Line in 1974, and can vividly remember opening the sleeper blind at dawn and beholding a wilderness through the window, a wilderness I would now recognise as Druimuachdar! Carelessly, I somehow allowed a quarter of a century to fly by before experiencing the line again - though at least my second trip was done in style, on the footplate of an EWS Class 66 General Motors diesel locomotive, racing through the Highland night with time sensitive Safeway containers. But it has not been until the last two or three years that I could claim to have come to know the railway between Perth and Inverness well. Well enough to realise that it is one of the United Kingdom's most dramatic and historic routes, a main line and a scenic railway all rolled into one; a spellbinding combination. The Highland Railway's publicity department evidently felt similarly: 'The scenery traversed by the Highland Railway far surpasses in interest and variety that on any railway route in the UK.' They didn't mince words in the corporate guide books of yesteryear. Hamilton Ellis was equally enthusiastic: 'It had the dignity and significance of a great railway, and though for long hours its stations slumbered in remote quiet, there were other times when enormous trains followed one another, dinfully shouting their passage through the high hills.'

Regrettably, those long trains are long gone, and modern rolling stock - with the honourable exception of ScotRail's Caledonian Sleeper and GNER's Highland Chieftain - is generally perceived as lacking the drama of its predecessors. It was unforgivable that so many classic Highland Railway locomotive designs were allowed to go to the breaker's torch without a single example being preserved. Apart from the Glasgow Museum of Transport's 'Jones Goods', official indifference has robbed railway enthusiasts of such handsome classes as the Bens, Castles, Lochs and Clans, some of the most beautiful machines ever to operate on a British railway.

Railways - however organic they may come to be seen in terms of the landscape they traverse - are seldom matters of a single impulse. What we now call the Highland Main Line is made up of four separate entities: the Scottish Midland Junction between Perth and Stanley, opened in 1848; the Perth & Dunkeld Railway of 1856; the Inverness & Perth Junction

Railway of 1863; and the Highland Railway's Aviemore to Inverness shortening completed in 1898. Naturally, dates and facts like these will strike little resonance with tourists, but they do reveal that the line we travel today was over half a century in the building, and that its impact was not an overnight sensation, not so much a single Napoleonic gesture, as a sequence of independent advances on the Highlands, a region so sparsely populated that railway promoters had, by definition, to be dreamers of dreams rather than coherent men of money driven solely by the profit motive.

The same holds true today. Paralleled for its entire course by the A9 trunk road, there are Philistines in high positions of power who would argue that the railway is obsolete and irrelevant. They miss the point. Though built for profit, and though miraculously surviving the profit blinkered inquisitions of Beeching and Serpel, the Highland Main Line's contribution at the dawn of the twenty-first century should be measured by its capacity to carry people and goods without impinging negatively on the environment. The main road, characterised by irritable bowel syndrome wracked processions of lorries, cars and caravans will never be able to emulate such innocence. It intrudes on the straths and glens of the Tay and Tummel, and on the wild open expanses of Druimucahdar and Slochd like a strip-o-gram interrupting a service in a Presbyterian Chapel, whereas the railway's passage is sublime and unintrusive. And no use arguing it wasn't conceived as such. Joseph Mitchell, the Inverness & Perth Junction's engineer, had the highly charged aesthetic conscience of a Ruskin - even though Ruskin himself abhorred railways and did his best to prevent a line being built through the Highlands! Inver, Dalguise and Killiecrankie are Mitchell's enduring monuments, the monuments of a Highlander at one with his heritage.

Contractors, Blair Atholl

James Shuttleworth

A steam special attacks Druimuachdar

What I am trying to get over to you is, I guess, that when you travel over the Highland Main Line, you should do so with a spirit of adventure. You are wasting a wonderful opportunity if you treat the train as simply a means to an end. It's that old Robert Louis Stevenson (who knew the line well) thing about 'travelling hopefully'. Attendance, on an increasingly regular basis, at Highland Rail Partnership meetings in Inverness, brought familiarisation as a dividend - though never contempt! My bathroom cabinet is overflowing with Caledonian Sleeper toothbrushes, disposable razors and face flannels. To be awakened by the rhythmic roll of the sleeper climbing past Dalnaspidal has become one of my great delights, and to end a day of hard concentration with a haggis supper and an Adnams in the Lounge Car one of life's great rewards.

Specifically for the preparation of this guide, I was able to ride in the cab of a ScotRail Turbostar over the line. These units are about as 'high tech' as trains

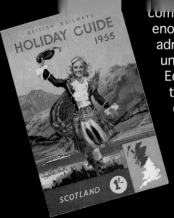

come these days, and though I am reactionary enough in railway matters to prefer 'real' trains, I admit to a good deal of admiration for these units. Accompanied by ScotRail's Paul Marrs, Edward Wallace and George McKenzie, I had a thoroughly enjoyable day, and learned much concerning present day operations on the Highland Main Line. As we journeyed southwards, climbing with comparative ease to Slochd, Paul and Eddie nostalgically recalled their early experiences as secondmen on English Electric Class 40s, staggering up to the summit at walking pace with the York Motorail in the mid Seventies. You see, even twenty-five years ago the railway was a different place, and there is little doubt that in a similarly future timespan folk will be dewy-eyed remembering Class 158s and HSTs.

Of course, there are some prepared to forecast that there will be no railways in the Highlands in 2027, but I am confident that the Highland Rail Partnership will prevent such dire consequences from ever coming to fruition. The HRP is an affiliation of bodies with the welfare of the railway system close to their hearts - councils, enterprise agencies, train operating companies and Railtrack, all who own to the shared aim of safeguarding and developing the lines north of the Highland Boundary Fault. Recent success stories include re-opening of Beauly station and the introduction of timber loading facilities at Kinbrace on the Far North Line; winter Sunday trains to Kyle and Wick; and inward oil flows to Lairg and Fort William. Modestly, I must add the publication of the 'Iron Road' guidebook series as an HRP cachet.

Contrasting with my Turbostar cab-riding experiences on the main line, I was fortunate to be shown over the Strathspey Railway on the footplate of an English Electric Class 20, a veteran of 1958, and a machine very much at home in the Highlands. On a blustery but sunny March day, Strathspey's Chairman, Doug Scott, and his colleague Graham Law, drove me to Broomhill and back, proudly introducing me to their lovely line. And what struck me most about the Strathspey Railway was the sheer amount of work undertaken by its largely volunteer workforce. Seeing senior citizens diligently repairing coaching stock on a wintry day - when they might well have been at home with their feet up by the fire - brought home to me just how loved railways are and just how much satisfaction and sense of achievement being involved with them brings. I hope some of that involvement rubs off on you as you follow in my footsteps. Arguably, the Perth to Inverness route has attracted as much affection down the years as any main line in Britain. Here's a few lines from an anonymous piece of verse which seem to sum up its appeal

> Think of breakfast at Kingussie
>> Think of high Drumochter Pass
> Think of Highland breezes singing
>> Through the bracken and the grass
> Scabious blue and yellow daisy
>> Tender fern beside the train
> Rowdy Tummel falling, brawling
>> Seen and lost and glimpsed again

Michael Pearson

The publishers are extremely grateful to the following organisations who have sponsored and encouraged the publication of this guide.

HIGHLAND RAIL PARTNERSHIP

The Highland Rail Partnership is an association of Highland Council, Perth & Kinross Council, Argyll & Bute Council, ScotRail, Railtrack, EWS, Freightliner, Argyll and the Isles Enterprise, Lochaber Limited, Inverness & Nairn Enterprise, Ross & Cromarty Enterprise, Caithness & Sutherland Enterprise, Moray Badenoch & Strathspey Enterprise and the Friends of the Kyle, Far North and West Highland Lines. The Partnership aims to assist the development of passenger, freight and heritage rail business across the Highland area.

ScotRail is Scotland's national passenger train operator, providing over 95% of services north of the border. We run four types of service - suburban round Glasgow and Edinburgh, interurban linking the six Scottish cities, rural in the West and North Highlands and South-West Scotland, and the Caledonian Sleepers which link Inverness, Fort William, Aberdeen, Glasgow and Edinburgh with London. The suburban network supported by Strathclyde Passenger Transport is the largest outside London. The National Express Group commenced in April 1997 a seven-year franchise during which we have invested £200M in new and refurbished trains, including the 100 mph three-car £3M Turbostar trains which are used on selected services over the Highland Main Line. Other trains used on the route have been refurbished, with increased carrying capacity for cycles, which go free on all ScotRail routes, and the Sleepers now include wheelchair-accessible cabins and overnight seating. Many fares on the Highland Main Line have been reduced to give even better value for daytrippers. Our Freedom of Scotland Travelpass includes Caledonian MacBrayne ferries and some Scottish Citylink routes. ScotRail Shortbreaks are unaccompanied and escorted holidays whose venues include Perth, Pitlochry, Kingussie, Aviemore and Inverness. We operate all of the stations on the Highland Main Line, and are proud of the regard with which they are held in their local communities.

Anglo-Scottish train operator, Great North Eastern Railway Limited (GNER) runs long-distance, high-speed train services between Scotland, the North East of England, Yorkshire, the East Midlands and London Kings Cross. It is a wholly-owned subsidiary company of Sea Containers Limited within its Ferries, Trains and Ports division.

GNER operates 44 services a day to and from Scotland, serving 22 stations within Scotland including Inverness, Aviemore, Pitlochry, Perth, Stirling, Aberdeen, Dundee, Edinburgh and Glasgow. Since 1996, GNER has invested over £40 million in train and customer service improvements. It has increased services by 20 per cent and attracted 28 per cent more passengers.

Between now and 2005 GNER is investing over £100 million in an intensive programme of improvements which includes refurbished trains, more seats on its Aberdeen and Inverness services, new locomotives, enhanced security and better passenger facilities throughout its stations. This investment programme will build on the qualities that have already earned GNER an award-winning reputation and will deliver to GNER passengers a more effortless journey, with greater reliability, comfort and service.

Further details of GNER services are available from stations and GNER's telecentre on 08457 225 225. Tickets may also be booked via GNER's website at www.gner.co.uk

The Highland Council
Comhairle na Gaidhealtachd
SERVING The Highland Community

The Highland Council is one of 32 unitary councils in Scotland, providing a wide range of essential services to a population of 210,000 people. The area covered by the council is 10,000 sq miles - one third of the area of mainland Scotland. The council has the largest area of any council in Scotland and is one of the largest in Europe. This large area gives the Council major responsibilities for land, air and sea transport. The Highland railways make an important contribution to the integrated transport network of sparsely populated rural communities and also provide important links to the remainder of Scotland and the UK.

Moray Badenoch & Strathspey ENTERPRISE

Moray, Badenoch and Strathspey Enterprise is a local enterprise company which is part of the Highlands & Islands Enterprise (HIE) network. It has substantial powers and resources to achieve economic and social development results across a range of business, skills and community programmes. MBSE has offices in Forres and Aviemore and covers an area from Dalwhinnie to Keith. With a population of 97,000 people in other important conurbations like Grantown on Spey, Elgin, Kinloss, Lossiemouth and Buckie, it is one of the most densely populated areas in the HIE network.

EWS

EWS - English Welsh & Scottish Railway - is Britain's largest rail freight operator providing a key service for British industry. Daily train services link all parts of Britain with the rest of the country and Europe, and the Highland Main Line is a key artery of the EWS network. EWS have invested over £700 million in 280 new locomotives and 2,500 new wagons. Nearly 1,100 train services are operated a day by EWS, moving over 100 million tonnes a year in markets as diverse as coal, timber, cars and steel. On the Highland Main Line EWS moves foodstuffs, express parcels, cement, building materials, freezer components and petrochemicals, and is continually seeking new traffic flows.

PERTH & KINROSS COUNCIL

The Perth and Kinross Council area lies at the 'Heart of Scotland' straddling the Highland Boundary Fault. Set at the upper tidal reach of the River Tay, the City of Perth has long been a transport hub of national importance and, for the railway network, this includes the southern gateway to the 'Iron Road to the Highlands'. At three other historic locations in Perthshire - Dunkeld & Birnam, Pitlochry and Blair Atholl - the Highland Main Line has been at the centre of local life since the 19th century. Perth & Kinross Council provides a comprehensive range of Public Transport Guides and a Local Public Transport Map and these are available from the Council's Public Transport Unit at Pullar House, 35 Kinnoull Street, Perth PH1 5GD or by telephoning 0845 3011130.

Safeway

With 114 stores, Safeway is the market leader in Scotland and the fourth largest retailer in the UK. Environmental issues are very important at Safeway. As part of its drive to cut air and noise pollution, Safeway has turned to the railway to help it transport its daily deliveries of fresh foods to its Scottish stores at Inverness, Elgin, Thurso, Wick, Nairn, Buckie and Kirkwall. Transporting some 180 tonnes per day, Safeway is the only retailer in Scotland to carry goods by rail. This pioneering service was recognised in 2001, with Safeway Supply Division being awarded the "Queen's Award for Enterprise"

Highlands & Islands ENTERPRISE

The Highlands and Islands is a vast and diverse area stretching some 420 miles north to south. The task of the Highlands & Islands Enterprise Network (HIE) is to help create a strong, diverse and sustainable economy where quality of life is matched by quality of opportunity.

The Network has substantial powers and resources to aid economic and social development. It can finance businesses, provide factories and offices, develop and implement training programmes, assist community and cultural projects and undertake environmental renewal. Assistance and advice is delivered mainly through ten Local Enterprise Companies (LECs) based in the areas they serve. Efficient, accessible and environmentally sustainable transport is vital for the functioning of the economy. The HIE network, in conjunction with local authorities, the rail industry and others is, therefore, a major funder of the Highland Rail Partnership whose aim is to promote rail development in the area.

BP Grangemouth is comprised of three of BP's businesses - Exploration, Oil and Chemicals. BP's Forties Pipeline System, the North Sea's biggest oil transportation system, provides the complex with raw materials for refining and the manufacture of petrochemicals. The refinery has an annual capacity of around ten million tonnes of fuel products. The petrochemical plants form one of the most flexible petrochemicals operations in Europe. A Bulk Train Loading Terminal within the refinery transports fuels to centres in Scotland and England. The site recently received a Scottish Executive grant to build a new rail terminal as part of a package of measures designed to shift transportation of products from road to rail. BP tanker wagons currently travel over the Highland Main Line on their way to Lairg in Sutherland.

RAILTRACK Scotland

Railtrack in Scotland aims to work with its partners to give Scottish rail passengers and freight users more trains, in shorter journey times and a better overall experience of using the railway network.

It is our intention that railway stations will become important transport hubs within local communities, and that much of the decay of our national railway infrastructure will be redressed, paying heed to our heritage, social and environmental responsibilities.

As a leading player in the Scottish business community, Railtrack in Scotland takes its social and environmental responsibilities seriously and works with many groups and organisations in an effort to further build partnership links with local communities and lineside neighbours.

The glinting waters of Glen Truim

The Highland Main Line
Perth to Inverness

APPROACH Perth's massive, sprawling railway station with an open mind. Ignore the almost perpetual gloom, the unsympathetically awful Nineteen-Sixties booking hall, your inability to gain access to the once splendid Corinthian columned refreshment rooms. Marvel instead at its bewildering size, its faded glory (seen to better advantage in George Earl's narrative paintings of 1895, *Going North* and *Coming South*, which hang in the National Railway Museum) the echoes, the shadows, the long meaningful silences between trains. If there was money to rebuild it, two or three platforms and a booking hall the size of a street corner convenience store would suffice. Be grateful that the coffers are empty, the budget bereft, so that Sir William Tite's imposing architecture is unthreatened by that euphemism 'progress'.

Tite was an extremely successful and prolific architect with a thriving London based practice. Typical of many successful Victorians, he also found time to be the Member of Parliament for Bath, to be a director of several companies, and a school and hospital governor. His other railway stations range from the grandiose likes of Carlisle Citadel, Lancaster Castle and Southampton Terminus, to more modest wayside stations such as Beattock, Crewkerne and Barnes. Perth station dates from 1847. At one time it was jointly shared (though not equally in terms of revenue) by the Caledonian, North British and Highland railways. It reminds one of Carlisle and Lancaster in its strong Tudor overtones in styling. Parts of it could pass as an Oxbridge college. *Inspector Morse* might have been filmed here and no one the wiser. The entrance lies in the V between the lines to Dundee and Inverness, beyond which passengers are left to their own devices, having of necessity to find their own way around its rambling, barn-like nooks and crannies with the spirit of a 19th century explorer. Lucky you have a mobile with you. Brr, brr, brr, brr: "National Rail Enquiries, Darren speaking. Which station do you wish to travel from?"

"Perth."

"Which station do you wish to travel to?"

"Perth"

"Then what's the problem?"

"I'm lost!"

Leaving Perth seems like a sound decision. What has happened to the "fine suburbs of the Fair City" enthusiastically extolled by the *Highland Railway Handbook*? Replaced by industrial units and retail parks it appears. Even the usually

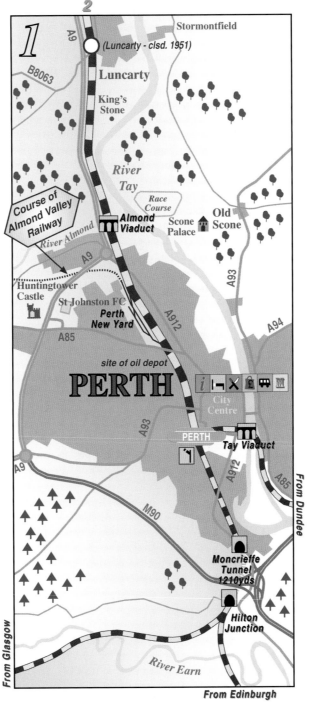

optimistic railway enthusiast won't find much consolation in the largely empty sidings of Perth New Yard, the result of a 1961 rationalisation programme replacing four outmoded yards dating from pre-Grouping times. Lacking in any inward freight flows, despatches of timber and bottled water take place from time to time. The survival of a turntable comes as a shock.

The railway through the Almond Valley to Methven and Crieff opened in 1858 and closed, to passengers at least, in 1951. Never exactly intensively operated, for many years the rump of the service was worked by a steam railcar. In its early years the railway almost made more money from carrying water supplies to the engine shed at Perth than passengers. On the extension to Crieff opened in 1867 the stations bore such evocative names as Madderty, Abercairney and Innerpeffray. Huntingtower Castle was once the home of William Whitelaw, one of the Highland Railway's most successful chairmen.

As the suburbs retreat, the Tay draws close. On the far bank, adjacent to Perth's National Hunt Race Course, you may catch a glimpse of Scone (say 'Skoon') Palace. This is a hugely significant place in Scottish history. Here, over the Stone of Destiny (or Lia Fail to give it its old Celtic name, for it is said to have originated from Ireland) the kings of Scotland were crowned until the stone was appropriated by Edward I in 1296 and taken to Westminster Abbey. There, apart from briefly being returned to Scotland in 1951, where it was hidden under the high altar of Abroath Abbey by an enterprising group of young Scots Nationalists, it remained until 1996 when it was placed in Edinburgh Castle. The present Palace of Scone is of early 19th century origin, being the family home of the Earls of Mansfield and open to the public throughout the summer.

The railway crosses the River Almond close to its confluence with the Tay. The Almond rises some thirty miles to the west in the neighbourhood of Ben Chonzie, passing picturesquely through the Sma' Glen on its travels. Its source is just a watershed away from Loch Tay, but the River Tay's journey to the outskirts of Perth is much the longer. A Roman Fort called Bertha stood at the meeting place of the two rivers.

Disappointingly masked by a cutting, though marked on the accompanying map, a standing-stone known as the King's Stone marks the site of a 10th century battle between the Scots and the Danes. Scotland's emblematic thistle is said to have derived from an invading Dane standing on a thistle and squealing in pain, loudly enough to wake the sleeping Scots.

Perth - Gateway to the Highlands

Stop
Look
Listen

Beware
of trains

AS far as Stanley Junction our way north lies over the route of the former Caledonian Railway, being part of its main line between Glasgow and Aberdeen. This stretch opened in 1848 as the Scottish Midland Junction Railway. The Highland Railway had running powers between Stanley and Perth which, incidentally, remains double track.

It was the Caledonian Railway - known affectionately as 'The Caley'- who operated the branchline to Bankfoot. Little chronicled, given even the esoteric nature of much of railway publishing, it opened in 1906. Its passenger services ran out of steam in 1931, though potatoes were carried for another thirty-three years. Bankfoot itself had its origins as a 19th century weaving village, now it's home to the Perthshire Visitor Centre and 'Macbeth Experience'.

Standing stones litter the landscape, evidence clearly of early occupation hereabouts in the history of man. Stanley was a textile community, its massive cotton mills originally established by Arkwright. They closed in 1989 but the Tayside buildings have been splendidly redeveloped for domestic use by the Phoenix Trust. The railway station was a three platform affair at the bifurcation of the Inverness and Aberdeen routes and dated from the opening of the Perth & Dunkeld Railway in 1856. Rather unusually, Highland trains used the island platform's inner (eastern) face when travelling northbound, and its outer (western) face in the opposite direction, a practice which enabled southbound trains to stand at the platform whilst awaiting a path into Perth on the main line. It would have been good to stand here in Edwardian times, admiring the stately passage of 'The Caley's' Prussian blue locomotives and red and white rolling stock in contrast with the Highland's homogeneous trains of olive green. It would have been equally rewarding to loiter on Stanley's platforms on 14th September 1966 when Sir Nigel Gresley's last streamliner, A4 No. 60024 *Kingfisher* was borrowed from the scrap line to work a Glasgow to Aberdeen 'Three Hour' express for the last time.

Main line? Not anymore. The Caledonian route through Strathmore to Forfar and Aberdeen was stripped

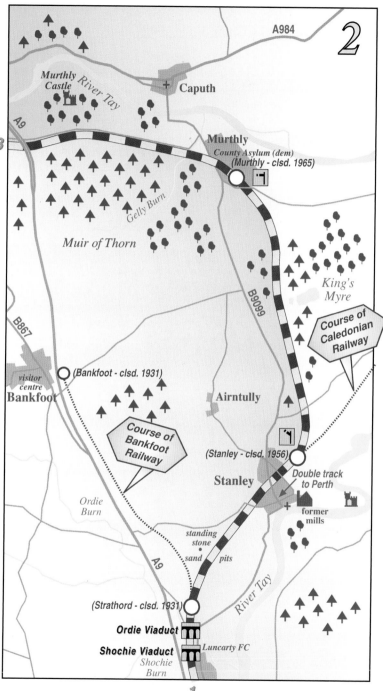

of its status in 1967, thereafter being little more than a lengthy siding retained for the occasional desultory goods. So nowadays, Stanley is only a junction in the sense that the line to the north singles at this point, overlooked by an impressively modern signal box of such recent provenance as 1961. Incongruous now, it looks like an aircraft control tower overlooking a deserted wartime aerodrome.

North of Stanley Junction we are on the Highland Line proper, traversing a heathland landscape bounded to the east by the meandering Tay. A lochan called King's Myre remains inarticulately tight-lipped as to the origins of its name. Then woodlands recede to reveal Murthly, one of numerous wayside stations which closed on 3rd May 1965 as a direct result of the Beeching Report. The two-platformed station has vanished, though happily its characteristic lattice footbridge has been preserved by the Scottish Railway Preservation Society and re-erected at Bo'ness. New light in old lanterns so to speak.

The Victorians often juxtapositioned asylums and railways, branchlines being built to facilitate the transfer of goods if not passengers, deranged or otherwise. Murthly was Perthshire's County Asylum, a siding ran into the grounds and was used by coal wagons bringing fuel for the hospital's power plants. Now it is in the throes of being demolished and redeveloped for housing. Too late, as one wit remarked, for the siding to be re-laid for a new generation of asylum seekers!

Murthly Castle has a history which spans the centuries, part of it dated back to the 1300s. One of its 19th century owners was Sir William Drummond Stewart, an inveterate traveller who returned from his travels with many treasures and antiquities, none more unusual than two live Red Indians who lived in a pagoda in the grounds. The castle itself, which Sir William hoped would rival Blair Atholl, was never completed, being largely demolished after the Second World War. No.145, one of the Highland Railway's powerful 4-6-0 locomotives, built in 1900 to the design of Peter Drummond, was named *Murthly Castle*. The class was so successful, that an order for fifty machines was placed by the Ouest Railway of France.

WHY does the scenery change so suddenly, so dramatically? It's the Highland Boundary's 'fault' - with an Iron Road guide you don't just get facts, you get great wit into the bargain. Yes, it's the Highland Boundary Fault slashing diagonally across Scotland from Bute to Stonehaven, polarising the environment into contrasting schisms of lowland and highland landscapes. Kingswood Tunnel contributes to the theatricality of the scene change, beyond its narrow bore the railway enters the Pass of Birnam just as stray lines from Shakespeare's 'Scottish' play begin to enter your head.

> "Macbeth shall never vanquished be, until
> Great Birnam Wood to high Dunsinane Hill
> Shall come against him."

Dunsinane is a dozen miles east south east of BirnamWood and, not unnaturally, Macbeth felt safe in his castle, whole woods, he reasoned logically, were not going to move themselves en masse. The denouement, of course, was that King Malcolm had his force of attackers camouflaged by foliage cut from the trees of Birnam Wood.

There was briefly a private platform for the laird of Rohallion Lodge. It didn't last long, perhaps because trains only stopped on Fridays! When this part of the line opened as the Perth & Dunkeld Railway in 1856, the original terminus was known as Birnam rather than Dunkeld, Birnam being the smaller of the two neighbouring communities sited on either bank of the Tay. Services quickly settled down to three trains in each direction between Perth and Birnam, a fourth being added in summer. Little time elapsed before the railway's excursion potential was realised. Factory workers from Perth were regularly introduced to the delights of the Highland scenery. For most trains, Dunkeld & Birnam (as it is now known) is the first port of call north of Perth. For seven years it marked the northerly terminus of the line. The imposing station building which you encounter today is the original of 1856, though it has lost its overall roof and there is no longer an engine shed, let alone a goods yard. Yet the station, designed by Andrew Heiton Jnr., retains its architectural dignity, look at the delicate ironwork which holds up the canopy, and the impressive stone chimneys which tower above the roof. John Kinnard was the first stationmaster here, and he has recently been immortalised by having a new auditorium at the Birnam

Institute named after him. Incidentally, the 'up' starting signal at the southern end of the station is unique in its retention of a Highland Railway finial. A mechanical signal box overlooks the station loop. The 'up' line is bi-directional and most frequently used by stopping trains in either direction. Dunkeld used gas lighting until 1982, and is thought to have been one of British Rail's last stations to do so.

In 1892, at the age of twenty-six, Beatrix Potter, the writer and illustrator of childrens books, came on holiday to Birnam with her family and her pet rabbit Benjamin Bunny who did not enjoy the overnight journey by train from King's Cross. Their rented accommodation at Heath Park (organised on their behalf by John Kinnaird!) overlooked the station. Her father must have been a nascent enthusiast: 'The trains prove to be a source of constant amusement,' she wrote in her diary. 'Papa is constantly running out, and looks out of the bedroom window at night.'

The line switchbacks up out of Dunkeld and down over the River Braan into Inver Tunnel. The decorated bridge over the Braan is well worth going to see if you are staying in the neighbourhood. On foot it forms a picturesque approach to Strathbaan with riverside walks up to The Hermitage, inspiration for a number of paintings by the Pre-Raphaelite, Sir John Millais, who was a friend of Beatrix Potter's father. The celebrated Scots fiddler Neil Gow was born at Inver in 1727. Two miles of level running along the alluvium terraces of Strath Tay lead to the site of a former station at Dalguise. The Duke of Atholl planted the neighbouring ridges by firing exploding canisters of seeds from a canon. Seek professional advice before trying this method at home. The timber-built station building at Dalguise remains, and again the creator of *Peter Rabbit* would have been familiar with this station, as her father leased nearby Dalguise House as a holiday home between 1871 and 1882. Beatrix was much taken with the then relatively new railway. 'Some people can see no sentiment or beauty in a railway. To my mind there is scarcely a more splendid beast in the world than a large Locomotive. I cannot imagine a finer sight than the Express, with two locomotives, rushing down this incline at the edge of dusk.'

The viaduct which carries the railway across the Tay at Dalguise is one of Joseph Mitchell's handsome structures, his response to the aesthetic challenge imposed is a mark of genius. Now you are on his Inverness & Perth Junction Railway of 1863, a hundred miles of mountainous railway constructed within just two years. An engineering miracle! Look out for fishermen in the river, thigh high against the flow in capacious waders.

Map labels:

4

B898 / A9

3

Dal-guise

Dowally

Dalguise Viaduct

Clachan More

(Dalguise - clsd. 1965)

Craigvinean Forest

Craig a Barns 1106ft

Forest Walks

A923

Cathedral / **Dunkeld**

Inver / Telford's Bridge / **Birnam**

Inver Tunnel 350yds

Forest Walks

The Hermitage / River Braan

Inver Viaduct

Beatrix Potter Exhibition

DUNKELD

loop

Birnam Hill

Kings Seat 1324ft

Rohallion Castle

Birnam Wood

River Tay

A984

A9

Kingswood Tunnel 330yds

Stare Dam

(Rohallion - clsd. 1864)

B867

2

Dunkeld & Birnam

Scottish Tudor at Pitlochry

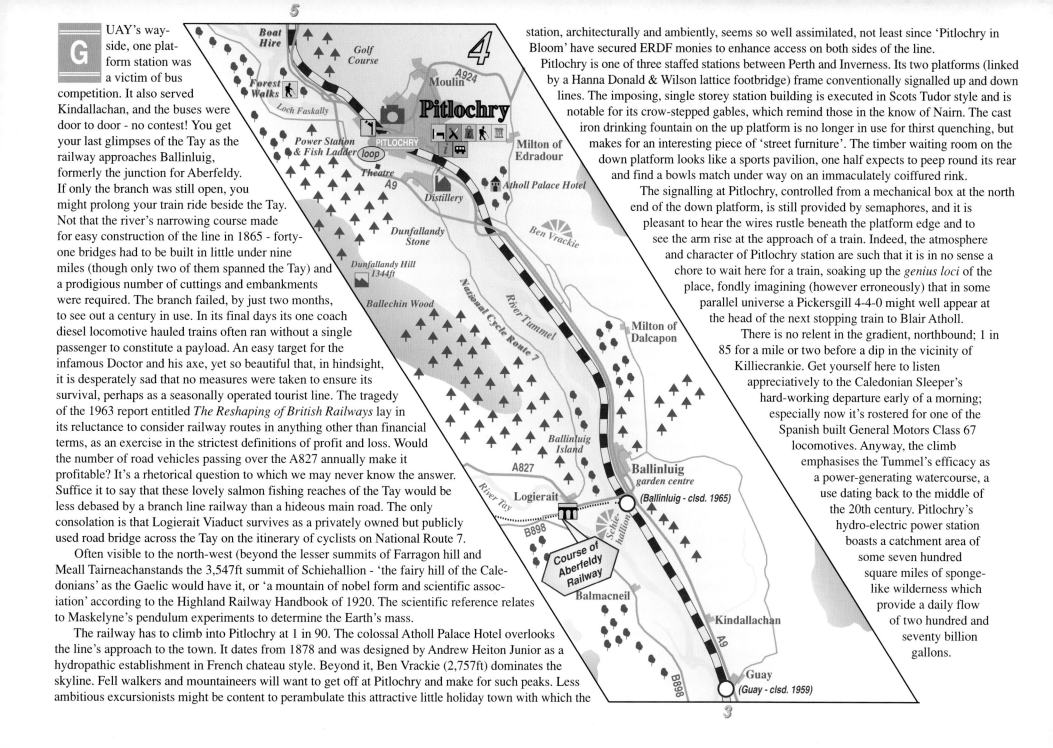

G UAY's wayside, one platform station was a victim of bus competition. It also served Kindallachan, and the buses were door to door - no contest! You get your last glimpses of the Tay as the railway approaches Ballinluig, formerly the junction for Aberfeldy. If only the branch was still open, you might prolong your train ride beside the Tay. Not that the river's narrowing course made for easy construction of the line in 1865 - forty-one bridges had to be built in little under nine miles (though only two of them spanned the Tay) and a prodigious number of cuttings and embankments were required. The branch failed, by just two months, to see out a century in use. In its final days its one coach diesel locomotive hauled trains often ran without a single passenger to constitute a payload. An easy target for the infamous Doctor and his axe, yet so beautiful that, in hindsight, it is desperately sad that no measures were taken to ensure its survival, perhaps as a seasonally operated tourist line. The tragedy of the 1963 report entitled *The Reshaping of British Railways* lay in its reluctance to consider railway routes in anything other than financial terms, as an exercise in the strictest definitions of profit and loss. Would the number of road vehicles passing over the A827 annually make it profitable? It's a rhetorical question to which we may never know the answer. Suffice it to say that these lovely salmon fishing reaches of the Tay would be less debased by a branch line railway than a hideous main road. The only consolation is that Logierait Viaduct survives as a privately owned but publicly used road bridge across the Tay on the itinerary of cyclists on National Route 7.

Often visible to the north-west (beyond the lesser summits of Farragon hill and Meall Tairneachanstands the 3,547ft summit of Schiehallion - 'the fairy hill of the Caledonians' as the Gaelic would have it, or 'a mountain of nobel form and scientific association' according to the Highland Railway Handbook of 1920. The scientific reference relates to Maskelyne's pendulum experiments to determine the Earth's mass.

The railway has to climb into Pitlochry at 1 in 90. The colossal Atholl Palace Hotel overlooks the line's approach to the town. It dates from 1878 and was designed by Andrew Heiton Junior as a hydropathic establishment in French chateau style. Beyond it, Ben Vrackie (2,757ft) dominates the skyline. Fell walkers and mountaineers will want to get off at Pitlochry and make for such peaks. Less ambitious excursionists might be content to perambulate this attractive little holiday town with which the

station, architecturally and ambiently, seems so well assimilated, not least since 'Pitlochry in Bloom' have secured ERDF monies to enhance access on both sides of the line.

Pitlochry is one of three staffed stations between Perth and Inverness. Its two platforms (linked by a Hanna Donald & Wilson lattice footbridge) frame conventionally signalled up and down lines. The imposing, single storey station building is executed in Scots Tudor style and is notable for its crow-stepped gables, which remind those in the know of Nairn. The cast iron drinking fountain on the up platform is no longer in use for thirst quenching, but makes for an interesting piece of 'street furniture'. The timber waiting room on the down platform looks like a sports pavilion, one half expects to peep round its rear and find a bowls match under way on an immaculately coiffured rink.

The signalling at Pitlochry, controlled from a mechanical box at the north end of the down platform, is still provided by semaphores, and it is pleasant to hear the wires rustle beneath the platform edge and to see the arm rise at the approach of a train. Indeed, the atmosphere and character of Pitlochry station are such that it is in no sense a chore to wait here for a train, soaking up the *genius loci* of the place, fondly imagining (however erroneously) that in some parallel universe a Pickersgill 4-4-0 might well appear at the head of the next stopping train to Blair Atholl.

There is no relent in the gradient, northbound; 1 in 85 for a mile or two before a dip in the vicinity of Killiecrankie. Get yourself here to listen appreciatively to the Caledonian Sleeper's hard-working departure early of a morning; especially now it's rostered for one of the Spanish built General Motors Class 67 locomotives. Anyway, the climb emphasises the Tummel's efficacy as a power-generating watercourse, a use dating back to the middle of the 20th century. Pitlochry's hydro-electric power station boasts a catchment area of some seven hundred square miles of sponge-like wilderness which provide a daily flow of two hundred and seventy billion gallons.

VIEWS - at least of the panoramic variety - are restricted as the railway plunges through the Pass of Killiecrankie. How frustrating that there is no longer a station to serve this famous beauty spot on the River Garry, with its National Trust visitor centre and associations with the battle of 1689 where 'Bonnie Dundee' routed General Mackay's English army. Killiecrankie's picturesque setting posed a challenge to Joseph Mitchell's imagination, but he proved himself more than equal to the task of negotiating the deep ravine in a functionally imaginative manner. The curving, ten arch, castellated viaduct and its adjoining tunnel appear to almost organically embrace the setting - perhaps best appreciated in the winter months when foliage and vegetation do not form an obstacle. So it is something of a challenge facing rail travellers to take in the rapidly passing scene of water glinting through trees, a widening pool, a rocky crag, and the 'Soldier's Leap', the last reputedly recalling a fear-induced jump of prodigious dimensions across the river by one of the defeated army attempting to escape. In a country more at ease with its bitter-sweet history, Killiecrankie would have been a mandatory stop on the railway to self-discovery. The National Trust for Scotland visitor centre offers interpretation of the neighbourhood and woodland walks. Significantly, the signal wires at Killiecrankie were carried on high posts to prevent them being affected by falls of snow. Marie Corelli (1854-1924), a dramatic and romantic authoress of considerable popularity in her age, spent a good deal of her time in Killiecrankie. The actual site of the Battle of Killiecrankie lay to the north-west of the pass on flatter ground. It proved a pyrrhic victory for Graham of Claverhouse (aka Bonnie Dundee) for he lost his own life in the short-lived fight and the Jacobite supporters of James VII failed to build on their victory over William of Orange's forces. Going under the A9, and emerging into a broader valley, the railway passes a quarry-worked hillside and crosses the River Tilt on yet another elegant and battlemented Mitchell viaduct before entering Blair Atholl. An experimental airplane was tested in Glen Tilt in 1907. Now an unstaffed halt but formerly a station of railway operating significance on the way to the summit of Druimuachdar, Blair Atholl retains some sense of importance, as the track doubles here for the twenty-three mile journey to Dalwhinnie. Trains are faced with a long, gruelling climb, climaxing at the ruling gradient of 1 in 70, to Druimuachdar. The engine shed, which in steam days provided banking engines, is still intact. It was brought stone by stone from Keith and re-erected at Blair Atholl. New sources of water had to be obtained from the

neighbouring hills for the servicing of locomotives, and Railtrack remain the providers of domestic supplies in the locality to this day. Snow plough fitted engines were another feature of railway operation here and it was also the turn-round point for local services from Perth. Nowadays many trains don't bother to stop at all, which (though an aid to express schedules) is disappointing for residents and tourists alike, let alone enthusiasts of railway architecture, for Blair Atholl, even if it no longer boasts a private waiting room for the Duke of Atholl, remains a stylish Inverness & Perth Junction Railway station overlooked by a charming timber-built signal cabin beside a level-crossing.

In company with the Garry, flowing west to east, the railway leaves Blair Atholl, steepening from 1 in 500 to 1 in 80. Initially, there are good views of the whitewashed ramparts of Blair Castle (home of Britain's only private army) to the north, but these give way to woodland and soon you are crossing the Water of Bruar just downstream from its famously picturesque waterfalls. Passing under the A9 you reach Struan, not the sort of station which you'd have backed to survive Beeching, but once again a disappointing casualty for ramblers and hill walkers, who might have found it a useful staging post, and for railway enthusiasts bent on obtaining a lineside view of the curious Calvine Viaduct, a three arched masonry structure on the down line with battlemented cutwaters, notable in that it spans the Garry and a road bridge across the river simultaneously. The 'up' line, put in in 1900, has a steel girder bridge. The train provides the briefest of views along Glen Errochty, the prominent peak to the west being Beinn a Chuallaich. Sturdy deer fences border the line, but the more wily beasts seem to get through!

5

6

River Garry

A9

Calvine

(Struan - clsd. 1965)
Struan   Calvine Viaduct

House of Bruar

Falls of Bruar

National Cycle Route 7

Beinn a Chuallaich

River Garry

Double track to Dalwhinnie

Water Mill

Blair Castle

River Tilt

Blair Atholl

Atholl Browse

BLAIR ATHOLL

Tilt Viaduct

Golf Course

Tulach Hill 1541ft

Quarry

A9

Killiecrankie

Craig Fonvuick 1345ft

(Killiecrankie - clsd. 1965)
Killiecrankie Tunnel 128yds

NTS Visitor Centre

Killiecrankie Viaduct

Meall Uaine

Pass of Killiecrankie

B8019

Craigower

Peter J. Robinson

An EWS Enterprise freight descends from Druimuachdar near Dalnaspidal

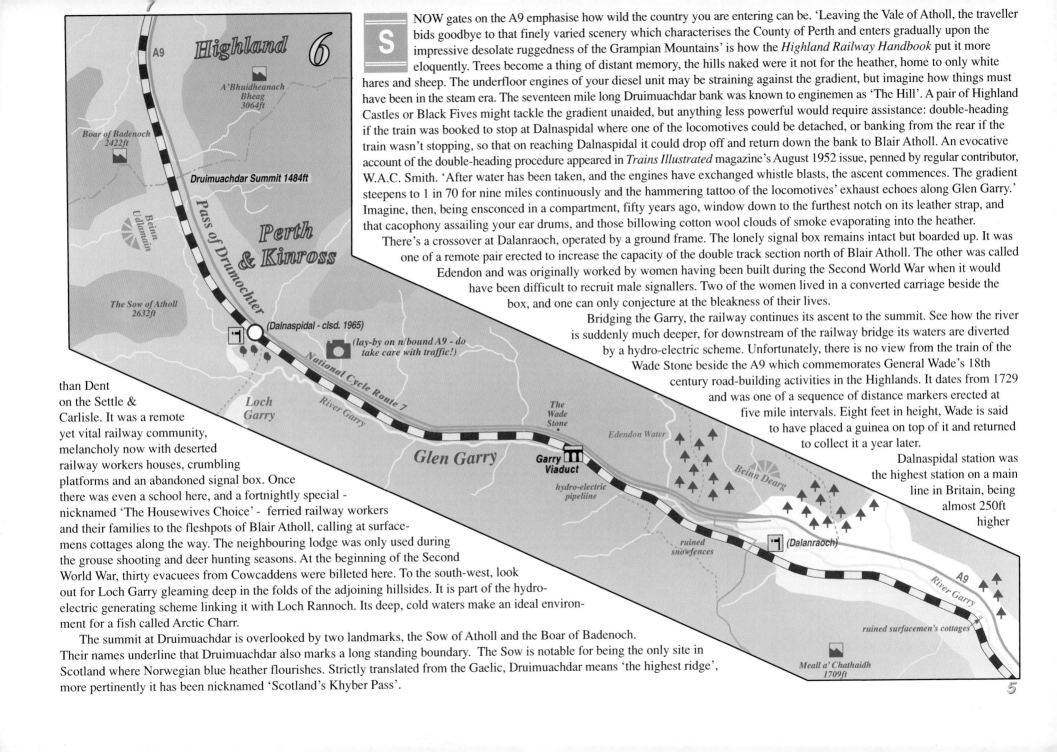

A'Bhuidheanach
Bheag
3064ft

Boar of Badenoch
2422ft

Druimuachdar Summit 1484ft

Beinn
Udlamain

Pass of Drumochter

*Perth
& Kinross*

The Sow of Atholl
2632ft

(Dalnaspidal - clsd. 1965)

National Cycle Route 7

(lay-by on n/bound A9 - do
take care with traffic!)

Loch
Garry

River Garry

Glen Garry

The
Wade
Stone

Edendon Water

*Garry
Viaduct*

hydro-electric
pipeliine

Beinn Dearg

ruined
snowfences

(Dalanraoch)

A9

River Garry

ruined surfacemen's cottages

Meall a' Chathaidh
1709ft

NOW gates on the A9 emphasise how wild the country you are entering can be. 'Leaving the Vale of Atholl, the traveller bids goodbye to that finely varied scenery which characterises the County of Perth and enters gradually upon the impressive desolate ruggedness of the Grampian Mountains' is how the *Highland Railway Handbook* put it more eloquently. Trees become a thing of distant memory, the hills naked were it not for the heather, home to only white hares and sheep. The underfloor engines of your diesel unit may be straining against the gradient, but imagine how things must have been in the steam era. The seventeen mile long Druimuachdar bank was known to enginemen as 'The Hill'. A pair of Highland Castles or Black Fives might tackle the gradient unaided, but anything less powerful would require assistance: double-heading if the train was booked to stop at Dalnaspidal where one of the locomotives could be detached, or banking from the rear if the train wasn't stopping, so that on reaching Dalnaspidal it could drop off and return down the bank to Blair Atholl. An evocative account of the double-heading procedure appeared in *Trains Illustrated* magazine's August 1952 issue, penned by regular contributor, W.A.C. Smith. 'After water has been taken, and the engines have exchanged whistle blasts, the ascent commences. The gradient steepens to 1 in 70 for nine miles continuously and the hammering tattoo of the locomotives' exhaust echoes along Glen Garry.' Imagine, then, being ensconced in a compartment, fifty years ago, window down to the furthest notch on its leather strap, and that cacophony assailing your ear drums, and those billowing cotton wool clouds of smoke evaporating into the heather.

There's a crossover at Dalanraoch, operated by a ground frame. The lonely signal box remains intact but boarded up. It was one of a remote pair erected to increase the capacity of the double track section north of Blair Atholl. The other was called Edendon and was originally worked by women having been built during the Second World War when it would have been difficult to recruit male signallers. Two of the women lived in a converted carriage beside the box, and one can only conjecture at the bleakness of their lives.

Bridging the Garry, the railway continues its ascent to the summit. See how the river is suddenly much deeper, for downstream of the railway bridge its waters are diverted by a hydro-electric scheme. Unfortunately, there is no view from the train of the Wade Stone beside the A9 which commemorates General Wade's 18th century road-building activities in the Highlands. It dates from 1729 and was one of a sequence of distance markers erected at five mile intervals. Eight feet in height, Wade is said to have placed a guinea on top of it and returned to collect it a year later.

Dalnaspidal station was the highest station on a main line in Britain, being almost 250ft higher

than Dent on the Settle & Carlisle. It was a remote yet vital railway community, melancholy now with deserted railway workers houses, crumbling platforms and an abandoned signal box. Once there was even a school here, and a fortnightly special - nicknamed 'The Housewives Choice' - ferried railway workers and their families to the fleshpots of Blair Atholl, calling at surfacemens cottages along the way. The neighbouring lodge was only used during the grouse shooting and deer hunting seasons. At the beginning of the Second World War, thirty evacuees from Cowcaddens were billeted here. To the south-west, look out for Loch Garry gleaming deep in the folds of the adjoining hillsides. It is part of the hydro-electric generating scheme linking it with Loch Rannoch. Its deep, cold waters make an ideal environment for a fish called Arctic Charr.

The summit at Druimuachdar is overlooked by two landmarks, the Sow of Atholl and the Boar of Badenoch. Their names underline that Druimuachdar also marks a long standing boundary. The Sow is notable for being the only site in Scotland where Norwegian blue heather flourishes. Strictly translated from the Gaelic, Druimuachdar means 'the highest ridge', more pertinently it has been nicknamed 'Scotland's Khyber Pass'.

WE have crossed the watershed, and now it is the River Truim, a tributary of the Spey, which accompanies the railway, not the Garry any longer. Beneath the blunt eastern flank of Geal-Charn, the train runs downhill at 1 in 80 past old railway workers' cottages at Balsporran to the end of the double track section at Dalwhinnie. This is wonderful country for hill-walkers and mountaineers, and much of the passenger business at Dalwhinnie station falls into this category, though first there is a tantalising view up Loch Ericht to tempt us. Field-Marshall Montgomery walked around the loch in 1944, making plans for D-Day.

As at Dunkeld, the main platform is bi-directional, which makes life easy for backpackers. The down Caledonian Sleeper, however, invariably uses the far, northbound platform, intriguingly dropping off deer-stalking figures of a morning, and as the train pulls out, you wonder what their day has in store for them. The somewhat austere and basic station building dates from the 1920s following rebuilding of the original after a fire - the Highland Railway appears rather careless with its buildings in this respect. At least the present station - the halfway point - offers protection from the elements on the frequently wild days that this part of the world appears to specialise in.

At 1,174 feet above sea level, Dalwhinnie lays claim to being Scotland's highest village. It was a centre for cattle droving in days gone by. Grateful to leave the inhospitable inn ("There was hardly anything to eat, and there was only tea, and two miserable starved Highland chickens, without any potatoes. No pudding and no fun.") Queen Victoria, journeyed over the pass in 1861, two years before the railway opened. "We passed many drovers without their herds and flocks, returning, we were told, from Falkirk." It was a sight the railway would eventually render extinct. For the best part of the ensuing century the most cost-effective way of moving cattle and sheep about was by rail.

Another industry grew up beside the railway line at Dalwhinnie, a business close to every Scotsman's heart - whisky making. Dalwhinnie Distillery opened in 1898, sited thus to make direct advantage of the transport facilities offered by the Highland Railway: coal and barley in, whisky out. The sidings remained busy until coal-firing ceased in 1961 and the maltings were rendered obsolete in 1968. A year later

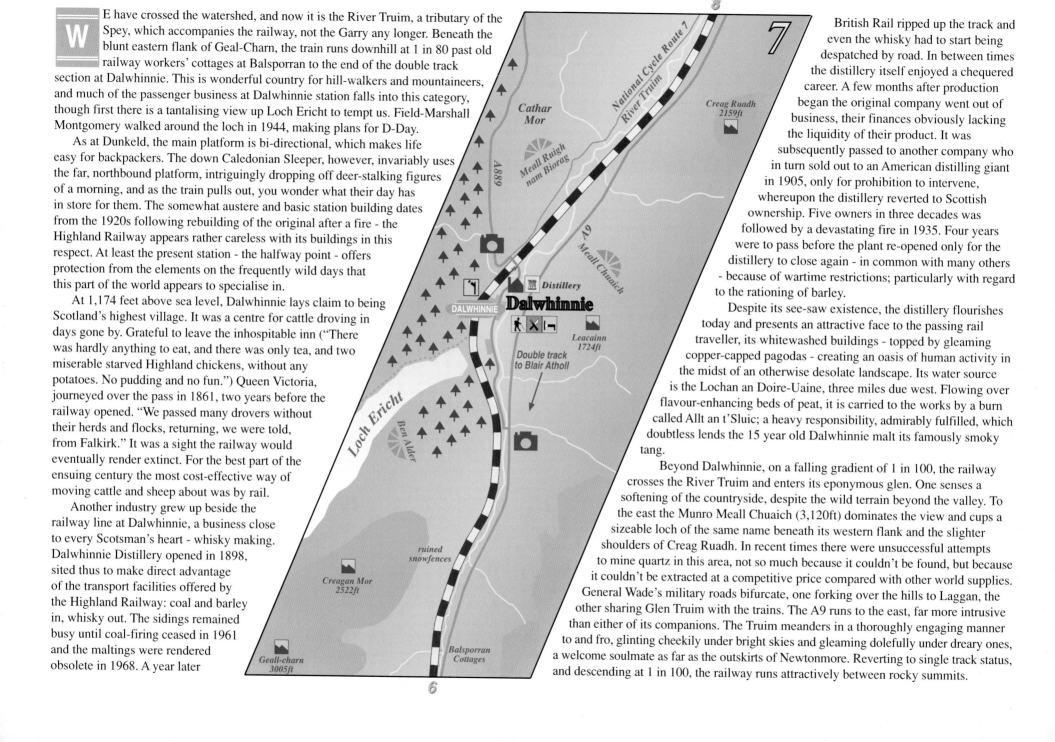

British Rail ripped up the track and even the whisky had to start being despatched by road. In between times the distillery itself enjoyed a chequered career. A few months after production began the original company went out of business, their finances obviously lacking the liquidity of their product. It was subsequently passed to another company who in turn sold out to an American distilling giant in 1905, only for prohibition to intervene, whereupon the distillery reverted to Scottish ownership. Five owners in three decades was followed by a devastating fire in 1935. Four years were to pass before the plant re-opened only for the distillery to close again - in common with many others - because of wartime restrictions; particularly with regard to the rationing of barley.

Despite its see-saw existence, the distillery flourishes today and presents an attractive face to the passing rail traveller, its whitewashed buildings - topped by gleaming copper-capped pagodas - creating an oasis of human activity in the midst of an otherwise desolate landscape. Its water source is the Lochan an Doire-Uaine, three miles due west. Flowing over flavour-enhancing beds of peat, it is carried to the works by a burn called Allt an t'Sluic; a heavy responsibility, admirably fulfilled, which doubtless lends the 15 year old Dalwhinnie malt its famously smoky tang.

Beyond Dalwhinnie, on a falling gradient of 1 in 100, the railway crosses the River Truim and enters its eponymous glen. One senses a softening of the countryside, despite the wild terrain beyond the valley. To the east the Munro Meall Chuaich (3,120ft) dominates the view and cups a sizeable loch of the same name beneath its western flank and the slighter shoulders of Creag Ruadh. In recent times there were unsuccessful attempts to mine quartz in this area, not so much because it couldn't be found, but because it couldn't be extracted at a competitive price compared with other world supplies. General Wade's military roads bifurcate, one forking over the hills to Laggan, the other sharing Glen Truim with the trains. The A9 runs to the east, far more intrusive than either of its companions. The Truim meanders in a thoroughly engaging manner to and fro, glinting cheekily under bright skies and gleaming dolefully under dreary ones, a welcome soulmate as far as the outskirts of Newtonmore. Reverting to single track status, and descending at 1 in 100, the railway runs attractively between rocky summits.

IEBALD moorlands give way to a wooded glen overlooked by rocky outcrops - don't let anyone ever tell you that Scotland's highland scenery is monotonous; there are rich subtleties which pay dividends on repeated visits. From the railway ledge above the Truim there's a glimpse of an elderly, double-arched bridge at Crubenmore, and a typical shooting box sheltering amidst trees. Almost on the point of collapse in the 1970s, the two hundred year old bridge was rebuilt by Borstal boys. The river tumbles over the Falls of Truim and the railway, descending steeply at 1 in 95 from Etteridge to the outskirts of Newtonmore, does its best to mimic the watercourse's gushing ways.

The railway builders must have experienced some relief to drop out of their mountain passes into the comparatively easy country of Strathspey, though that was not immune to difficulty, on account of the river's propensity to flood. Creag Dhubh, jutting dramatically above birch woods to the west, is a popular crag with climbers. On its southern flank is a cave used by Cluny Macpherson in 1746 to hide from Government troops after the debacle of Culloden. He remained in hiding for eight long years before escaping to France where, homesick for his glens, he died in 1756. By all accounts he was a wily fox. On one occasion whilst visiting friends in the neighbourhood he was surrounded by a party of redcoats. Displaying typical native cunning he dressed quickly as a servant and went out and offered to hold the officer's horse while the soldiers searched the premises. The ruse succeeded and he was delighted to be tipped for his trouble! Not inappropriately, 'Creag Dhubh' is the Clan Macpherson battle cry.

In a surprisingly soft, meadowland setting, the Truim forms a confluence with the famous River Spey two miles south-west of Newtonmore. At this point, to all intents and purposes, you are in the centre of the Scottish Highlands. The Spey remains friends with the railway as far as Aviemore. At ninety-eight miles, it is Scotland's second longest river and is as well known as the Tweed, the Tay and the Clyde. A substantial girder bridge spans the river half a mile south of Newtonmore station. Originally this was a wooden structure. The present bridge dates from 1885 and, as you will see from the east side of the train, was formerly double tracked.

Hardly three miles separate Newtonmore from Kingussie and we should be grateful, perhaps, that in the days of railheads and rationalisations, both stations survived. Newtonmore did less well out of the deal, being shorn of its loop and staffed status. Waiting on a cold night for the London bound sleeper here now means huddling in a bus shelter until its headlight gilds the metals, for the station building has become a private residence.

A golf course occupies land between the railway and the river on one side, whilst you would be forgiven believing that you had suddenly been caught in a time warp as, lineside to the west, the train runs past the rare breeds and preserved buildings of the Highland Folk Museum's prestigious Newtonmore site. It gives you every excuse to alight at Kingussie (the 'g' is silent by the way) and visit both locations which this admirable museum has to offer.

At 745ft above sea level, Kingussie's staffed and well kept station serves a small town with a faintly metropolitan air about it in the context of these unpopulated glens. Michael Chaplin, creator of BBC Television's popular Sunday evening drama, *Monarch of the Glen,* was first inspired to work on the project after the train he was on stopped here one morning in 1968. Furthermore, we are now deep in shinty country, that peculiarly Scots game that has been described as hockey with attitude. Kingussie - who play in red and blue hoops - are one of the sport's premier clubs and their history goes back as far as 1893. Their ground, known as The Dell, lies just over the level crossing.

Kingussie station building itself, an 1894 replacement of the original Inverness & Perth timber structure, is typical of Highland Railway architecture, and once contained some substantial refreshment rooms. Part of it is now in private use; handsome side screens protect you from winds funnelled down the strath. A large modern school, which has the unfortunate look of a factory about it, stands beside the line as the train pulls away from Kingussie and crosses the River Gynack. In the grounds of the neighbouring Folk Museum you'll see a typical highland 'black house' and a clack mill. Away to the east, prominent on a bluff of high ground beyond the A9 stand Ruthven Barracks, last fought over during the Jacobite Rebellion of 1745.

Kingussie

Folk Museum

Ruthven Barracks

B970

River Spey

loop

shinty

A9

Newtonmore

Folk Museum

River Calder

shinty

golf course

Spey Viaduct

8

Creag Dhubh

Spirean Beag
1951ft

National Cycle Route 7

River Spey

River Truim

Loch Etteridge

Falls of Truim

Cruban Beag
1935ft

Crubenmore Bridge

Glen Truim

Meall Ruigh nam Biorag
1780ft

Meall Odharaich
1743ft

A9

DECEPTIVELY idyllic, this was a difficult stretch of railway to build on account of the boggy nature of the terrain in the flood plain of the Spey. Variations in gradient are minimal - a somewhat atypical characteristic where the Highland Main Line is concerned - and in the neighbourhood of milepost 75 the track is actually level for some distance, and passed for 100mph running. To combat the soggy nature of the ground the line was reputedly laid on a raft of sheep's bladders! Badenoch, the name given to the district, means, appropriately the submerged or drowned land. It may look serene on a still morning with the mist rising from the reedbeds of the valley floor, but this has always been a difficult area when it comes to flood control. In the summer of 1829 the river rose seventeen feet above its normal level. Three thousand people were rendered homeless and effectively destitute. Some sheep, the fortunate ones, were rescued from treetops when the water subsided. During the winter of 1892 the line between Kingussie and Kincraig, carried across the Insh Marshes on an embankment some ten feet high, was washed away. An obelisk, somewhat masked by trees between Lynchat and Balavil, commemorates the Macpherson family. James Mcpherson, the poet and translator of Gaelic verse, is buried in Westminster Abbey.

Nowadays Insh Marshes are an important nature reserve looked after by the Royal Society for the Protection of Birds who recognize this mysterious landscape as perhaps the most significant flood plain wetland environment in Britain. Certainly the view through the carriage window is excitingly different from all those mountain ranges we have grown used to. Horizoned by the Monadhliath (Mon-a-lea-a) Mountains to the west and the Cairngorms to the east, the Spey meanders across the marshes before pouring into Loch Insh, the remnant of a much bigger expanse of water which filled the valley floor thousands of years ago. Up to two hundred whooper swans from Iceland winter on the marshes. Red squirrels hoard hazel nuts in the autumn. Redstarts, tree pipits and wood warblers nest here in spring. In summer the wild orchids have to be seen to be believed. All of which makes one wish there was still a station at Kincraig to detrain on a whim at and melt into the landscape. It closed in 1965 and only a passing loop remains. Originally it appeared in the timetable as Boat of Insh, reflecting the name of the neighbouring community and its ferry across the Spey before the road bridge was built.

The loop has a 'now you see it, now you don't' sort of history, being originally installed in 1882, removed in 1966, and reinstated in 1979. Along with Dunkeld and Kingussie, a camping coach was stabled at Kincraig for a number of years. How good it would have been to holiday here, with the mountains at your beck and call, the marshes for judicious exploration, the Spey to fish upon, and the continual interest of the passing railway scene to be absorbed.

The River Feshie adds its not inconsiderable waters to the Spey just downstream of Loch Insh. The river and its mountainous hinterland were favourites of the artist Sir Edwin Landseer, a regular visitor to the vicinity. Queen Victoria passed through Glen Feshie in 1861 and wrote enthusiastically of 'how enchanting it would be to live in such a spot'.

Forestry impairs some of the otherwise panoramic views to be had from the train of the neighbouring Cairngorms. There are summits within striking distance which rear up to four thousand feet and beyond. They tower above a protective rampart of Munros. Sgor Gaoith (the windy peak) is, at 3,658ft, the highest point on the ridge which parallels the railway. Beyond it rise such giants as Cairn Toul (4,241ft), Braeriach (4,248ft) and Ben Macdui (4,296ft). In comparison, the Monadhliath Mountains to the west appear somewhat less charismatic.

The railway passes between Loch Alvie and the adjacent hill of Tor Alvie on which no less than three monuments commemorate historic figures and events. Most prominent of these is a 90ft high granite column dedicated to the memory of the Duke of Gordon aka the 'Cock of the North' who died in 1836. A less conspicuous monument remembers the Duke's mother, a popular figure locally, especially with 'would be' soldiers who she encouraged to join the Gordon Highlanders by providing them with a 'kiss and a shilling'. She and her husband raised a good number of children, no small number of them without the aid of their spouse. At one time they had two sons called George, a potentially confusing situation solved by the Duchess referring to the boys as 'the Duke's George' and 'my George'. The hill's third monument salutes those Gordon Highlanders who fell at the Battle of Waterloo. Briefly, the Spey wanders away from the railway to sidle round the eastern flank of Tor Alvie. It can't, however, bear to be away for long, and is reunited as it heads towards Aviemore.

A9
B9152
B970
Loch Alvie
Alvie
Duke of Gordon's Monument
Waterloo Cairn 1175ft
Duchess of Gordon's Monument
River Spey
Moor of Alvie
loop
Kincraig (Kincraig- clsd. 1965)
Loch Insh
Watersports Centre
B970
Craigbui Wood
Wildlife Park
9
Macpherson's Monument
Balavil
Nature Reserve
Lynchat
A9
cemy. B9152
8
Insh Marsh
The Dell of Killiehuntly
i RSPB Reserve
Drumguish
B970

Peter J. Robinson

Aviemore's capacious wooden station

Aviemore
An Aghaidh Mhor
SCOTRAIL

Tourist Information
Catholic Church
Youth Hostel
Nature Reserve
Tennis Courts
ROTHIEMURCHUS
COYLUMBRIDGE
GLENMORE
THE CAIRNGORMS

Ticket Office

STATIC caravans and timber holiday homes characterise the railway's southern approach to Aviemore, one of the best known tourist centres in the Scottish highlands. The railway deserves the credit (though some would say the blame) for kick-starting Aviemore's development following the creation of a junction here when the direct route between Inverness and Aviemore opened in 1898. A new station was built to cope with anticipated increases in traffic. Quite unlike any other Highland Railway station, this symphony in timber is the work of Murdoch Patterson. We might not have had it still to admire, had not the Aviemore Partnership come to its rescue as, approaching its centenary and in considerable decay, British Rail proposed the easy option of demolition. Considerable refurbishment ensued, revealing a wonderful 'strawberry cheesecake' of a building: all mouth-melting creams, biscuit umbers and fruity reds; a real pleasure to saunter around, especially safe in the knowledge that a steam hauled train may soon appear and whisk you metaphorically away to another age. A small, but nice touch is the provision of replica Highland Railway nameboards. And not only is the infrastructure congenial - in 2001 Aviemore won ScotRail's 'most passenger friendly medium sized station' award.

When it was built the station's most important function was to facilitate the splitting and joining of portions, the practice being to run services as one train up from Perth, and divide them at Aviemore into two parts, one of which would proceed via the new direct line to Inverness, while the other ambled around the old, circuitous route via Forres and Nairn, a journey which took over an hour longer. Perhaps this method of working led to the confusion of the elderly lady in an oft quoted Highland Railway tale. Soon after the northbound train she was on started away from Aviemore the guard appeared and asked her where she was going:

"Nane o' your business," she replied.

"But I'm the guard," explained the official, "I have to ken where a'body's going."

"Well," sniffed the old lady, "if you must know I'm going to Inverness."

"That's fine then," said the guard, taking his departure.

"Whit dae ye think o' the impudence o' that mannie?"

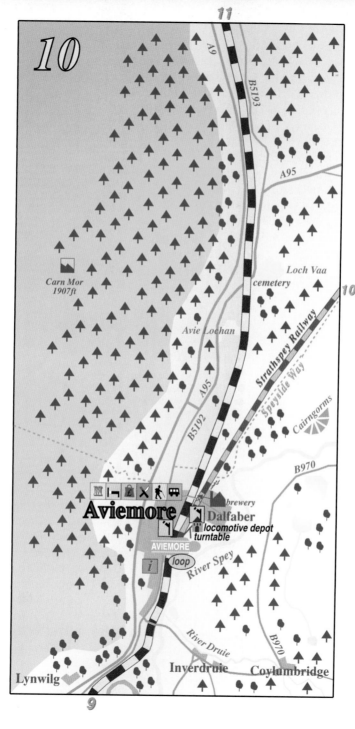

the old lady asked of the other passengers in her compartment. "Asking me where I'm going. Damned cheek! But I fooled him. I told him I was going to Inverness but I'm not going to Inverness at all. I'm going to Perth!"

Following closure of the Forres line in 1965 (with typical irony, at a time when Aviemore itself was being developed into an altogether more pro-active tourist resort) Aviemore station's purpose in life diminished and the infrastructure deteriorated. Happily, refurbishment has brought a good deal of activity back to the station which is now a centre of focus for a number of activities: sports shop, restaurant, estate agent plus, of course, the ScotRail and Strathspey Railway booking offices.

The original and direct routes went their different ways at the north end of Aviemore station. Via the old summit at Dava it was 60 miles to Inverness, the new route almost halved the distance. In contrast to the speed with which the Dunkeld to Forres section was constructed, the direct line took eight years to build. Reading between the lines, one suspects the Highland Railway's heart wasn't really in it. Money was 'too tight to mention', and they probably wouldn't have bothered building it at all, had it not felt threatened by competition from the North British Railway, who were again agitating for a new route to Inverness through the Great Glen. Resurrected by the Strathspey Railway, the illusion of a junction remains, though now it is sadly no longer possible to traverse the old main line with its bleak summit of 1052ft.

Leaving the valley of the Spey, the railway begins to climb, steepening to 1 in 150 as it journeys through woodland interspersed with fish rich lochans. Between the trees there are good views eastwards to the incomparable Cairngorms - how can you square it with your conscience, to be passing by and not call in. Now, even railway enthusiasts have no excuse, for the region's newest railway can be found ascending Cairn Gorm itself in the shape of a two kilometre long, two metre gauge funicular line opened in December 2001 to improve transport facilities without compromising the environment. The rolling stock is Swiss built and it takes twelve minutes to make the journey to the top. The funicular can be seen on clear days from trains on the main line, a bold vertical stroke on the mountainside to the east.

10A

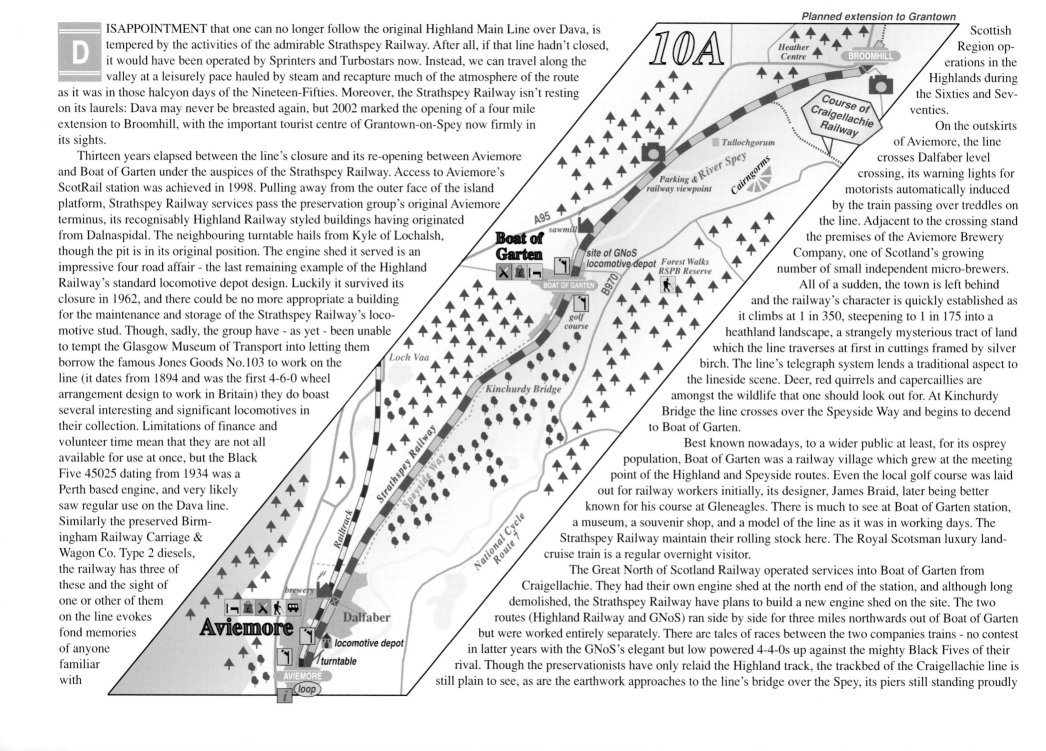

DISAPPOINTMENT that one can no longer follow the original Highland Main Line over Dava, is tempered by the activities of the admirable Strathspey Railway. After all, if that line hadn't closed, it would have been operated by Sprinters and Turbostars now. Instead, we can travel along the valley at a leisurely pace hauled by steam and recapture much of the atmosphere of the route as it was in those halcyon days of the Nineteen-Fifties. Moreover, the Strathspey Railway isn't resting on its laurels: Dava may never be breasted again, but 2002 marked the opening of a four mile extension to Broomhill, with the important tourist centre of Grantown-on-Spey now firmly in its sights.

Thirteen years elapsed between the line's closure and its re-opening between Aviemore and Boat of Garten under the auspices of the Strathspey Railway. Access to Aviemore's ScotRail station was achieved in 1998. Pulling away from the outer face of the island platform, Strathspey Railway services pass the preservation group's original Aviemore terminus, its recognisably Highland Railway styled buildings having originated from Dalnaspidal. The neighbouring turntable hails from Kyle of Lochalsh, though the pit is in its original position. The engine shed it served is an impressive four road affair - the last remaining example of the Highland Railway's standard locomotive depot design. Luckily it survived its closure in 1962, and there could be no more appropriate a building for the maintenance and storage of the Strathspey Railway's loco-motive stud. Though, sadly, the group have - as yet - been unable to tempt the Glasgow Museum of Transport into letting them borrow the famous Jones Goods No.103 to work on the line (it dates from 1894 and was the first 4-6-0 wheel arrangement design to work in Britain) they do boast several interesting and significant locomotives in their collection. Limitations of finance and volunteer time mean that they are not all available for use at once, but the Black Five 45025 dating from 1934 was a Perth based engine, and very likely saw regular use on the Dava line. Similarly the preserved Birm-ingham Railway Carriage & Wagon Co. Type 2 diesels, the railway has three of these and the sight of one or other of them on the line evokes fond memories of anyone familiar with

Scottish Region op-erations in the Highlands during the Sixties and Sev-venties.

On the outskirts of Aviemore, the line crosses Dalfaber level crossing, its warning lights for motorists automatically induced by the train passing over treddles on the line. Adjacent to the crossing stand the premises of the Aviemore Brewery Company, one of Scotland's growing number of small independent micro-brewers.

All of a sudden, the town is left behind and the railway's character is quickly established as it climbs at 1 in 350, steepening to 1 in 175 into a heathland landscape, a strangely mysterious tract of land which the line traverses at first in cuttings framed by silver birch. The line's telegraph system lends a traditional aspect to the lineside scene. Deer, red quirrels and capercaillies are amongst the wildlife that one should look out for. At Kinchurdy Bridge the line crosses over the Speyside Way and begins to decend to Boat of Garten.

Best known nowadays, to a wider public at least, for its osprey population, Boat of Garten was a railway village which grew at the meeting point of the Highland and Speyside routes. Even the local golf course was laid out for railway workers initially, its designer, James Braid, later being better known for his course at Gleneagles. There is much to see at Boat of Garten station, a museum, a souvenir shop, and a model of the line as it was in working days. The Strathspey Railway maintain their rolling stock here. The Royal Scotsman luxury land-cruise train is a regular overnight visitor.

The Great North of Scotland Railway operated services into Boat of Garten from Craigellachie. They had their own engine shed at the north end of the station, and although long demolished, the Strathspey Railway have plans to build a new engine shed on the site. The two routes (Highland Railway and GNoS) ran side by side for three miles northwards out of Boat of Garten but were worked entirely separately. There are tales of races between the two companies trains - no contest in latter years with the GNoS's elegant but low powered 4-4-0s up against the mighty Black Fives of their rival. Though the preservationists have only relaid the Highland track, the trackbed of the Craigellachie line is still plain to see, as are the earthwork approaches to the line's bridge over the Spey, its piers still standing proudly

Heather Centre — BROOMHILL

Course of Craigellachie Railway

Tullochgorum

River Spey

Parking & railway viewpoint

Cairngorms

A95

sawmill

Boat of Garten

site of GNoS locomotive depot

Forest Walks RSPB Reserve

BOAT OF GARTEN

B970

golf course

Loch Vaa

Kinchurdy Bridge

Strathspey Railway

Speyside Way

Railtrack

National Cycle Route 7

brewery

Dalfaber

Aviemore

locomotive depot

turntable

AVIEMORE

loop

i

in the face of the often swollen waters of the Spey. Notice how the countryside has changed dramatically since Boat of Garten, far more open and undulating now, typical of the riparian farmland of Speyside, you could be forgiven for thinking you had passed into Aberdeenshire. The river meanders close to the railway, and ospreys can occasionally be seen helping themselves to a fish, much to the chagrin of fishermen who pay well to cast their lines along these beats. Back when the Highland and GNoS lines ran parallel here, the tracks had different colours of ballast! The Cairngorms provide an imposing backdrop to this charming scenery. A prominent V shaped gash in their bulwark-like face is called Lairig Ghru, and it takes some stretch of imagination to accept that the Great North of Scotland Railway once sounded a proposal to build a line through this pass to link Strathspey with upper Deeside and their Ballater branch. The farm at Tullochgorum became famous in Scottish country dancing circles by lending its name to a Strathspey reel.

A mile beyond the former 'junction' for the Criagellachie line the old Highland Railway line reaches Broomhill. Out in the wilds on the west bank of the river, this was considered the station for Nethy Bridge, almost two miles away on the far side of the Spey. A horse and trap provided what we would now refer to as 'integrated' transport. The Strathspey Railway would ideally like to revive the link to give some credence to Broomhill as a 'terminus' pending another extension of the line, with Grantown-on-Spey as the desired objective.

Meanwhile, Broomhill should prove popular with the tourists, for it doubles as 'Glen Bogle' for filming purposes connected with the popular television series *Monarch of the Glen*.

The original station building was demolished following closure of the line, but a replica Highland Railway structure has been erected, together with a 'by request' signal with semaphore arms which could be operated by prospective passengers to stop passing trains. The stationmaster's house remains intact. It belongs to the Strathspey Railway Company and is leased to one of a total of six full time employees. Two disused surfacemen's cottages nearby may be converted for use as holiday homes.

In its original form, Broomhill didn't have (or need) a run-round loop, so the preservationists have built one beyond the platform. Service trains pass through the platform, run round and then pull back into the platform to let passengers off. As soon as is practical, work on relaying the track towards Dulnain Bridge and Grantown will commence. A bridge has to be rebuilt over the River Dulnain and a new 'tunnel' expensively provided at Gaich in connection with road improvements on the A95. Grantown's handsome Highland Railway station was demolished (though, ironically, the GNoS building survives) and new structures occupy the trackbed, so a brand new station will need to be built to serve the town. Judging by their determination and success to date, any difficulties encountered will be overcome by the Strathspey Railway and their volunteers.

The Strathspey Railway's Caledonian Railway McIntosh 0-6-0 No. 812 (built in Glasgow in 1899) waits to leave Aviemore.

deep, 350,000 cubic yards of waste were excavated to allow the line to reach its second summit. More dramatic than Druimuachdar, if no more desolate, Slochd was - according to the reliable High-land Railway guide book - the 18th century haunt of robbers and bandits. Regular travellers will tell you that you can discern the face of a soldier in the adjoining rock. A bi-directional loop, cont-rolled by Aviemore signal box, offers useful passing facilities and you may find yourself waiting here for a few minutes: time to ponder on the trains ability to introduce you to the wilderness and at the same time protect you from it.

At 1 in 60 the line drops down from Slochd to Strath-dearn and the whisky-distilling village of Tomatin. A lovely view opens up south-westwards along the valley of the River Findhorn which the railway curves to cross on arguably the line's most handsome bridge, a graceful structure - designed by Murdoch Patterson - of nine steel trusses supported by tapering masonry piers. From a train it produces the feeling of flight. Seen from below it wonder-fully harmonises with its gorgeous riverine setting. Nothing could be more photogenic yet, despite being easily accessible by road, it rarely features in the railway press.

Tomatin Viaduct, an imposing though less dramatic structure than its more flam-boyant neighbour, carries the line high above the smoking chimney tops of Tomatin village to the site of the station. Ninety-nine miles from Perth, its loop remains, together with a disused wartime signal box, but the pretty timber station building, similar to that at Carrbridge, has been demolished. As at Dalwhinnie and Kingussie, Tomatin Distillery had its own private siding which in this instance remained in use until the 1970s. Nowadays the much enlarged distillery is in Japanese ownership, though the ten year old malt it makes remains highly regarded. Leaving Tomatin behind, there are good views to the east of the River Findhorn wending its way towards its outfall beyond in the Moray Firth beyond the town of Forres.

THE Highland Line conquers its second major summit, Slochd, 1,315 feet above sea level, a five mile ascent from Carrbridge, two miles of it at a taxing 1 in 60. Surrounded by conifer plantations, the line approaches Carrbridge, the penultimate station these days before Inverness is reached. The loop at Carrbridge station is bi-directional and services often pass here. The station building is an attractive timber original. Immediately beyond the platforms the railway runs loftily over the River Dulnain, a tributary of the Spey which rises on Beinn Breac in the Monadhliath Mountains. Shortly afterwards a much more modest watercourse is spanned by a seemingly unnecessarily substantial bridge. Not so, this was the scene of the Highland Line's most tragic incident when, on June 18th 1914, following a sudden cloud burst over the neighbouring hills, Baddengorm Burn became a twenty foot high wall of water which pierced the railway embankment, creating a yawning gap some fifty feet long at the bottom and one hundred and twenty feet long at the top. As fate would have it, the 11.50am Highland Railway train from Perth to Inverness was just pulling away from Carrbridge at 3.25pm as the bridge and embankment were hit. Three carriages in the middle of the train were washed away and five people were drowned. It was an extraordinary disaster which could hardly have been forseen. The storm had thrashed about the slopes of Carn Glas for less than an hour. Yet the hailstones were said to be the size of "pigeon's eggs" and the burn "extraordinarily turbid and the consistency of pea soup". Astonishingly, the bridge was rebuilt in twenty-five days; McAlpines were the contractors and two hundred men involved in the work. Nine years later history repeated itself at this spot - if anything more damage being done - though fortuitously, on this occasion, no trains were passing.

The station at Carrbridge is 914ft above sea level and the railway has to climb four hundred feet in five or so miles to reach the rocky summit at Slochd. You cannot escape the sense of climbing as even the conifer plantations are left behind, Slochd's curving viaduct (with adjoining surfacemen's cottages) traversed, and the curving ascent to Drumbain cutting accomplished: fifty-six feet

Map labels

Funtack Burn
R. Findhorn
River Findhorn
A9
Tom na h-Ulaidh 1238ft
R. Findhorn
(Tomatin- clsd. 1965)
distillery
loop
Tomatin
Tomatin Viaduct
Findhorn Viaduct
National Cycle Route 7
A9
Carn nam Bain-tighearn 2082ft
loop Slochd Summit 1315ft
Drumbain Cutting
Slochd Viaduct
Carrbridge
A938
Dulnain Viaduct loop
Landmark Centre
CARR BRIDGE
River Dulnain
A9

I N one sense it's downhill all the way to Inverness, yet metaphorically it's not downhill at all, there being much still to savour and enjoy over the last fifteen miles between Moy and this particular journey's end.

Sadly, Loch Moy is all but hidden from the railway by woodland. Similarly Moy Hall, famous seat of the Clan Mackintosh, the present house dating from the 1950s, the original being a castle built upon an island in the loch in the 14th century. Moy is chiefly remembered as the scene of a 'rout' in 1746, when a large body of Government troops, in pursuit of Bonnie Prince Charlie, were turned back by the local blacksmith and four other men whose wild Highland yelps from the woods were sufficient to fool the Hanoverian force that a much larger body of Jacobites was ranged against them. Bonnie Prince Charlie was quartered at Moy Hall with Colonel Anne Mackintosh, a spirited female supporter of the cause whose husband was somewhat inconveniently a captain in the opposing ranks of the Black Watch. After the defeat at Culloden, Lady Anne was held prisoner and taken to Inverness where some amongst the victorious English would have had her hanged. Her great charm and beauty is said to have saved her from such a fate!

Moy station survives as a private residence, its gable ends typically crow-stepped and thistle-topped whilst the initials HR and the date 1896 are still engraved in its handsome stonework. George V and Lloyd George used the Mackintosh's private waiting room here in 1921. The current owners breed Siberian huskies.

A long curving embankment carries the line across an area of boggy ground bordering the Moy Burn. There are speed restrictions as the railway crosses the Aultnaslanach Viaduct, the only timber built bridge on a main line in Scotland. Murdoch Paterson is said to have employed a wood called 'green heart' because firm foundations could not be sunk into the neighbouring ground. In summer clumps of meadow-sweet emphasise the wet nature of the local terrain. Railtrack have voiced plans to retire this unique structure, moving it gracefully to the side and replacing it with a new bridge of steel.

We cross the watershed between the Findhorn and the Nairn. By milepost 105 the signalling jurisdiction changes from Aviemore to Inverness. Conifer plantations close in,

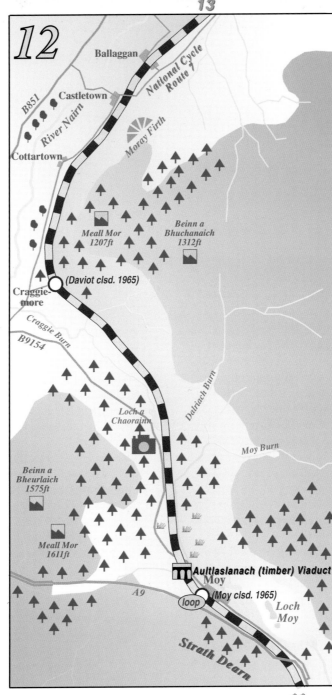

followed by a mile or so of cuttings, restricting views. The A9 has moved to the west, making a more direct approach to Inverness

Set on a curve in a rocky cutting, the remains of the platforms are still just about discernible at Daviot, originally the penultimate stop on the line and the point at which the track re-doubled. As at Tomatin the buildings, which they closely resembled, have been demolished, but look out for the ruined base of the old water tower. The village it purported to serve lies a convoluted country mile to the west on the far bank of the River Nairn and is chiefly notable for its 18th century church, the design of one Thomas Telford.

Escaping from the trees, the line offers views westwards across the River Nairn towards the Moray and Beauly firths and a mountainous horizon beyond. After the moorland wastes we have become accustomed to, it is reassuring to be reintroduced to farms, small holdings and domestic dwellings which encroach upon the railway, materialising in small communities like Cottartown, Castletown and Ballaggan. The Nairn runs off the shoulders of Beinn Bhuidhe to the south-west of Daviot and runs for some thirty miles to outpour into the Moray Firth.

An intriguing account of the direct route's impact on this part of the Nairn valley appears in Neil T. Sinclair's 1998 book *The Highland Main Line* (Atlantic Publishers). The author's father had grown up on a farm beside the new railway as it was being built, whilst his grandfather had been forced to negotiate with the Highland Railway for compensation over loss of crops and with regard to the siting of accommodation bridges. At the last minute, the Highland Railway decided to double the track as far south as Daviot and a number of bridges in the vicinity had to be widened before even being used. A thrill in those days was to watch southbound expresses being double-headed out of Inverness on the long climb up to Slochd. The railway brought subtle changes in its wake. Hitherto the locals had relied on peat cut from the neighbouring hillside for heating fuel. Thereafter it became easier to collect coal from the station yards at Daviot and Culloden Moor. Also with the railway came new opportunities for employment in a previously agriculturally reliant community. For sixty years the railway became an integral part of life beside the River Nairn until Beeching stepped in and closed the local stations.

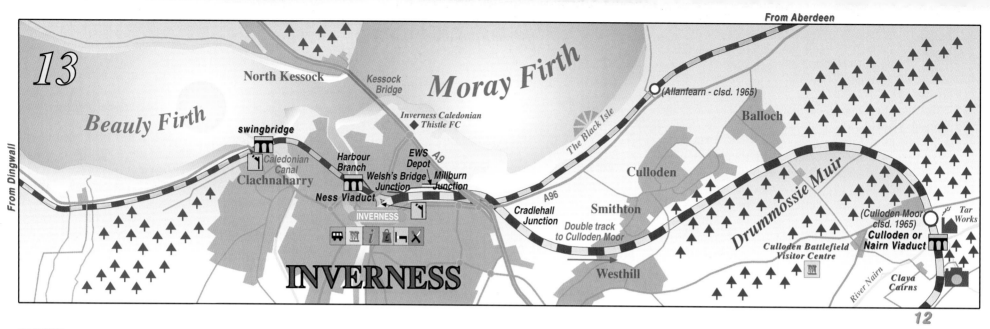

13

Beauly Firth

North Kessock

Kessock Bridge

Moray Firth

(Allanfearn - clsd. 1965)

Balloch

Inverness Caledonian Thistle FC

The Black Isle

swingbridge

Caledonian Canal

Clachnaharry

Harbour Branch

EWS Depot

A9

Culloden

Welsh's Bridge Junction

Millburn Junction

Ness Viaduct

A96

Drummossie Muir

INVERNESS

Cradlehall Junction

Smithton

(Culloden Moor clsd. 1965)

Tar Works

Double track to Culloden Moor

Culloden or Nairn Viaduct

INVERNESS

Culloden Battlefield Visitor Centre

Westhill

River Nairn

Clava Cairns

A S if it has been keeping it up its sleeve for maximum effect, the Highland Main Line saves its biggest bridge for its last, the Culloden (or Nairn) Viaduct being a massive 29-arch red sandstone structure 600 yards long, the widest river span being 100ft in length and 128ft above the River Nairn. Photogenically, it's at its best near dawn or sunset when the sun's red rays add lustre to the viaduct's masonry. A fresh bank of deposited stone at the southern end of the viaduct shows where washout damage had to be repaired in April, 2000, closing the line for three weeks. In the wide valley below stand Calva Cairns, a notable group of standing stones thought to date from between 1500 and 2000 BC. The track becomes double again towards the north end of the viaduct, though this is nothing more than a headshunt now, and a disused one at that, since the neighbouring tar works no longer relies on rail use. But the line does double as it passes the site of Culloden Moor station and stays so all the way down into Inverness. In Highland Railway and LMS days the station nameboards urged passengers to alight here for the battlefield of the same name. Nowadays tourists must get to the scene of the 1746 Jacobite defeat (only a mile west of the railway) by road. The line circumnavigates the field of battle - the last significant military action ever fought on British soil - not out of respect, so much, as the need for the railway engineers to effect a workable gradient out of Inverness.

At 1 in 70 the line descends through swarthy cuttings of tall grasses and ferns bounded by dense plantations of conifer trees. Intermittently the cuttings fall away and bring worthwhile views across the Moray Firth to the Black Isle. In fine weather you may even see as far as Ben Wyvis which overlooks the Kyle of Lochalsh line west of Dingwall. Gradually new pockets of housing begin to underwrite the suburban fringe of Inverness and your fellow travellers begin to stir and gather up their belongings. Be grateful you're not a Jacobite

survivor of the Battle of Culloden, rounded up and being taken into Inverness to be shot against a wall. Fast food restaurants, a cinema complex and sundry retail parks reassure you that you are inhabiting a more peaceful, if less resonant, century. Vaulting over the single track line from Aberdeen, your train skims the muddy margin of Moray Firth, passes a far from salubrious landfill site, dives beneath the A9's dual carriageway approach to the Kessock Bridge of 1982, and reaches Millburn Junction, formal meeting point of the Aberdeen and Perth routes, alongside an interesting (even if you're no trainspotter) array of sidings given over to freight activity, the stabling of EWS locomotives (and snowploughs!) and a carriage wash.

In Highland Railway times a ticket platform stood outside the main station for the purposes of revenue protection. Here also stood Welsh's Bridge which gave access to Millburn House. Welsh's Bridge is remembered by the name of the junction which leads to the Rose Street Curve which gives direct access to the Kyle of Lochalsh and Far North lines. Inverness's famous horse shoe shaped engine shed, whose turntable was approached through a triumphal water tank-bearing arch, closed in 1962, its site now occupied by a supermarket. Another victim of modernisation has been the Highland Railway Company's Lochgorm works, but at least ScotRail's maintenance plant - responsible for the upkeep of the Caledonian Sleeper fleet - continues to be busy.

The terminus dates from the opening of the Inverness & Nairn Railway in 1855 and, despite its modernised concourse - which echoes Perth in its gauche response to its Victorian surroundings - it forms a cohesive entity with the station hotel. Uniquely Y shaped, and still subject to interesting working practices involving train reversal, Inverness station provides a fittingly dynamic end to your journey, and one invariably accompanied by the plangent sound of seagulls calling overhead. What are they saying? Why "Failte don Gaidhealtachd", of course!

If there's a moral to this guide book at all, it is that you should not sit slavishly on the train, but that you should get off and explore the often achingly beautiful countryside it links you to. We are not Egon Ronay, we are not the Scottish Mountaineering Club, we are not the local Chamber of Commerce, all the facilities and suggestions listed in this gazetteer are by way of being ideas for your own personal development; points of departure if you prefer. To the best of our knowledge the entries are accurate at the time of going to press, but we would urge you to use the telephone or the internet to check ahead of your journey for your own peace of mind. Make good use of the local Tourist Information Centres who are unfailingly courteous and models of patience and humour in the face of the most inane tourist enquiry.

AVIEMORE   Map 10

One of the Highland's best known resorts, but far from typical of the region, Aviemore is a modern development which owes its tourist origins initially to the creation of a railway junction here in 1892 and subsequently the creation of winter sports facilites and the Aviemore Centre in 1966. A walk down its main street will fail to reveal overmuch Scots atmosphere - you could be forgiven for thinking you'd arrived in the Yukon - but there's no doubting its popularity with holidaymakers from all over the world.

Accommodation

CAIRNGORM HOTEL - Grampian Road. Tel: 01479 810233. Three star hotel across the road from the railway station.
HILTON AVIEMORE - Tel: 01479 810681. Four stars, within easy reach of the station.
YOUTH HOSTEL - Grampian Road. Tel: 01479 810345.
MOUNTAIN SUPPLIES BUNKHOUSE - Grampian Road. Tel: 01479 810903. Inexpensive accommodation from £10 per night.

Eating Out

HAMBLETTS - Grampian Road. Tel: 01479 810300. Comfortable modern restaurant serving Scottish and Mediterranean dishes just a few yards from the station - turn left!
HARKAI'S - Grampian Road. Tel: 01479 810430. Long established fish and steak restaurant.

ROYAL TANDOORI - Grampian Road. Tel: 01479 811199. Popular Indian restaurant.
WINKING OWL - Grampian Road. Tel: 01479 810646. Camra recommended pub.
MOUNTAIN SUPPLIES - Grampian Road. Tel: 01479 810903. Lively coffee shop above outdoor clothing and equipment outlet.

Shopping

Full range of facilities available along the main street within easy reach of the station: supermarkets, banks, clothing stores, outdoor equipment, crafts and souvenirs; plus an unusually good photographic shop (Tel: 01479 810371) for a town of this size.

Things to Do

TOURIST INFORMATION CENTRE - Grampian Road (2 minutes walk to left from station) Tel: 01479 810363.
STRATHSPEY RAILWAY - Aviemore Station. Tel: 01479 810725. Scenic steam train rides and wine & dine trains.
CAIRNGORM MOUNTAIN RAILWAY - Tel: 01479 861261. 9 miles east of Aviemore (bus connections). Exciting new funicular system offering breathtaking views of mountain scenery.
LOCH INSH WATERSPORTS - near Kincraig (Map 9) 7 miles by road from Aviemore. Tel: 01540 651272. Wide variety of water-based and general leisure activities: sailing, windsurfing, canoeing, mountain bikes, river trips, fishing, woodland trails, tuition and hire. Self catering and restaurant facilities.
AVIEMORE BREWERY - Dalfaber. Guided tours. Tel: 01479 811465.

Transport Connections

BUSES - Tel: 01463 702458.
CYCLE HIRE - Bothy Bikes. Tel: 01479 810111.
CAR HIRE - MacDonald's Self Drive - Tel: 01479 811444.

BIRNAM   Map 3

Leave the station, studiously ignoring the hurtling traffic on the A9 (which a subway spares you from in any case) and you drop down into a Birnam little changed from how it must have been when the first Victorian excursionists arrived. Perhaps Birnam would have grown much larger had not the railway been extended northwards, carrying travellers to even more sublime scenery. Some of Scotland's oldest and tallest trees feature in the abundant woodland. If you're walking on to Dunkeld, try not to miss the kirk at Little Dunkeld, where Neil Gow is buried.

Mr Tod, Beatrix Potter Garden, Birnam

Accommodation

BIRNAM HOUSE HOTEL - Perth Road. Handsome, medium-size, two star hotel handy for the station. Tel: 01350 727462.

Eating Out

BIRNAM INSTITUTE - Station Road. Tel: 01350 727674. The Foyer Cafe and Bistro Restaurant provide catering facilities of high quality. Recommended!
KATIE'S TEA ROOM - Perth Road. Coffees, teas and light meals en route from station to Dunkeld. Tel: 01350 727223.

Shopping

Post office (of unusual 'wild west' architecture and also offering teas), Spar general store, and a number of craft outlets.

Things to Do

BEATRIX POTTER EXHIBITION - Tel: 01350 727674. Beatrix Potter frequently holidayed in the vicinity and this fascinating exhibition celebrates her work and her keen interest in the locality. The adjoining garden features sculptures of a number of her animal characters.
THE HERMITAGE - National Trust for Scotland woodland walks located approximately 1 mile north-west of Birnam and Dunkeld. Good views of railway viaduct and tunnel mouth.

Transport Connections

CYCLE HIRE - Dunkeld Cycles, Perth Road. Tel: 01350 728744.
TAXIS - Ross's, Station Road. Tel: 01350 728828.

Walking

Undemanding signposted walks in the vicinity, notably an untaxing ascent of Birnam Hill. Shakespeare is said to have visited the area in 1601 and was obviously inspired! Leaflets available from the TIC in Dunkeld.

BLAIR ATHOLL   Map 5

A charming estate village in the shadow of Blair Castle. Robert Louis Stevenson stayed here in 1881 and wrote an amusing poem - in a parody of Robbie Burns' style - concerning the delights of Atholl Brose, a devastating cocktail of whisky, honey and oatmeal.

Accommodation

ATHOLL ARMS HOTEL - Tel: 01796 481205. Splendid traditional Scots two star hotel handily located a few yards from the station and the gates of Blair Castle.

Eating Out

BOTHY BAR - cosy annex to above featuring painting of Duchess of Atholl - the Stanier Pacific, not the lady! Beers from the Moulin Brewery.

THE LOFT - Tel: 01796 481377. Award winning bar and restaurant food.

Shopping

A general stores, post office and bank provide useful practical facilities, but Blair's outstanding establishment is the wittily named ATHOLL BROWSE, a mainly secondhand bookshop located beside the station and open most afternoons. Here bookworms may happily pass the time between trains. There's a particularly good choice of Scottish titles; whilst Nancy Foy (the owner) along with the bookbinding talents of her husband John Cameron (an ex professional railwayman) produces a fascinating range of self-published titles of largely local interest. Tel: 01796 481530.

Things to Do

BLAIR CASTLE - Tel: 01796 481207. Spectacular home of the Dukes of Atholl for over seven hundred years. The castle and its grounds are open to the general public from April to October and literally offers 'something for everyone' within its 2,500 acres.

WATER MILL - Tel: 01796 481321. Working exhibit with tea room.

MUSEUM - Tel: 01796 481232. Local history with refreshments.

HOUSE OF BRUAR - Tel: 01796 483236. Popular country retail outlet adjacent to Falls of Bruar walk. 3 miles north of Blair Atholl. Bus connections.

KILLIECRANKIE VISITOR CENTRE - National Trust for Scotland. Tel: 01796 473233. Interpretive centre (featuring model of railway viaduct) and departure point for some fabulous woodland walks. 4 miles south of Blair Atholl. Bus connections.

Transport Connections

BUSES - connections to Killiecrankie and Bruar. Tel: 0870 608 2 608.

TAXIS - Blair Atholl Garage. Tel: 01796 481221.

CYCLE HIRE - Atholl Mountain Bikes. Tel: 01796 473553.

BOAT OF GARTEN   Map 10A

Speyside 'resort' village which developed on the back of the railway junction. The name derives from the existence of a ferry over the river before the bridge was built. Best known now (apart from its steam trains) for its nesting ospreys.

Accommodation & Eating Out

THE BOAT - Tel: 01479 831258. Pleasant three star hotel beside the Strathspey Railway station. Bar and restaurant meals.

FRAOCH LODGE - Deshar Road. Tel: 01479 831331. Bunkhouse accommodation.

Shopping

Post office, general store (offering bike hire - Tel: 01479 831225) and excellent shop for fishermen called ALLEN'S - Tel: 01479 831372.

Things to Do

OSPREY CENTRE - Tel: 01479 831476. Located 3 miles west of the railway station. Access by way of Forest Walks.

Transport Connections

BUSES - fairly good Mon-Sat service links with Grantown-on-Spey and Aviemore. Tel: 01463 702458.

CARRBRIDGE   Map 11

Peaceful little resort which sprang up around the eponymous 18th century bridge whose ruined arch still picturesquely spans the Dulnain. Pleasant walk down from the station past the curling pond to the village centre.

Accommodation & Eating Out

THE CAIRN HOTEL - Tel: 01479 841212. Main Road. Homely three star hotel offering accommodation and bar food. Fish & chips across the road. Tea rooms and cafes.

CARRBRIDGE BUNKHOUSE - Dalrachney House. Tel: 01479 841250.

Shopping

General store, post office and chemist plus a number of craft, antique and souvenir outlets.

Things to Do

LANDMARK - Tel: 01479 841613. 'Fun, discovery and adventure for all ages' is how this increasingly popular centre markets itself. A miniature 'Alton Towers' for the Highlands would be an equally good description, but there are exhibits of a more thoughtful nature too: interpretations of forestry and wildlife to make you think amongst the fun. Recommended!

DALWHINNIE   Map 7

Wonderfully isolated settlement chiefly notable for its distillery. An ideal railhead for hill walkers and mountaineers, there being a classic route via Loch Ericht and Ben Alder to Rannoch or Corrour on the West Highland railway.

Accommodation & Eating Out

THE INN AT LOCH ERICHT - Tel: 01528 522257. Thankfully modernised since failing to amuse Queen Victoria in 1861, and now Dalwhinnie's sole establishment, 'The Inn' provides handy accommodation and eating facilities for visitors to this lonely outpost. 10 minutes walk from the station - turn right at the main road.

Things to Do

DALWHINNIE DISTILLERY - visitor centre (7 mins walk from station) open Mon-Fri March to December plus Saturdays June to October and Sunday afternoons in July and August. Tel: 01540 672219. Fascinating tours to be had of Scotland's highest distillery with a complimentary dram on offer at the end. Souvenir shop. Restrictions on children under 8 years old.

DUNKELD   Map 3

One of the most enjoyable places to stop along the line, Dunkeld is reached across Thomas Telford's graceful bridge over the Tay of 1809, and Scotland's longest river sets the scene for exploration of this lovely little town. Turn first left for The Cross (with its memorial fountain of 1866 and whitewashed 'little houses') and proceed to the ruined cathedral and the tomb of the Wolf of Badenoch. On fine days it's good to picnic on the banks of the Tay and watch the fishermen at work.

Accommodation

ATHOLL ARMS HOTEL - Bridgehead. Tel: 01350 727219. Very comfortable hotel in which Queen Victoria chose to put up on 11th September 1844. ROYAL DUNKELD HOTEL - Atholl Street. Two centuries old former coaching inn now a well appointed three star hotel. Tel: 01350 727322.

Eating Out

MACLEANS REAL MUSIC BAR - Tay Terrace. Tel: 01350 727340. Friendly bar noted for its 'stovies' and spontaneous outbursts of folk music. THE PINES - Atholl Street. Tel: 01350 727343. Coffee shop frontage to County Bakery.

Shopping

Bank, chemist, post office and food stores, plus good selection of craft and local produce outlets. Notably: the National Trust for Scotland's ELL SHOP by The Cross (an 'ell' being a weaver's measure of 39 inches) and ROBERT MENZIES grocery and wine merchants dating from 1795 on Atholl Street. KETTLES, again on Atholl Street, is an ironmongers with an eye for the tourist trade, whilst MACLEANS on Cathedral Street specialises in folk music, much of it recorded on its own label.
continued overleaf:

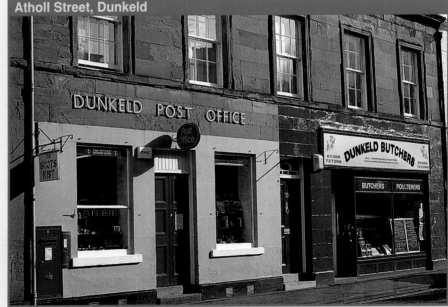
Atholl Street, Dunkeld

continued from previous page:

Things to Do
TOURIST INFORMATION CENTRE - The Cross, Tel: 01350 727688.

Transport Connections
BUSES - limited service links with Aberfeldy and Blairgowrie. Tel: 0870 608 2 608.

INVERNESS
Map 13

It must be hoped that Inverness's recently acquired city status doesn't go to the Highland capital's head. Already perfectly formed, there is scant need for spurious defining accolades, let alone unnecessary growth. Walk straight out of the station and the centre embraces you without formality. Saunter through the close-packed streets (which all, eventually, appear to lead to the riverbank) and you're likely to feel immediately at home. Not a lot of people know that Inverness is the only place outside of London where the Cabinet has met. We'll leave it to your curiosity to discover under what circumstances!

Accommodation
ROYAL HIGHLAND HOTEL - Station Square. Tel: 01463 231926. Former Station Hotel dating back to Highland Railway days and still redolent of that golden era though no longer do 'porters meet every train'! Three stars and not the most economical hotel in town but worth staying in for its grandiloquent atmosphere and proximity to the station.
GLEN MHOR HOTEL - Ness Bank. Comfortable three star hotel in riverside setting with good restaurants. Tel: 01463 234308.
TRAVEL INN - Millburn Road. Lodge style accommodation in hotel 10 minutes walk from railway station. Tel: 01463 712010.
YOUTH HOSTEL - Victoria Drive. 7 minutes walk from station off millburn Road. Tel: 01463 231771.

Eating Out
THE MUSTARD SEED - corner of Bank and Fraser streets. Open 12-3pm and 6-10pm daily. Lively and modern riverside restaurant which would not seem out of place in Edinburgh or Glasgow. Highly personable young staff serve memorable meals at surprisingly inexpensive prices. Tel: 01463 220220.
QISMAT TANDOORI - Millburn Road. Tel: 01463 716020. Indian restaurant near station.
THE AULD DISTILLERY - Millburn Road - informal 'Beefeater' restaurant adjunct to Travel Inn, overlooking railway sidings, ten minutes walk from

The River Ness at night

station. Tel: 01463 712010.
PALIO - Queensgate. Tel: 01463 711950. Pasta and pizza in pleasant surroundings.
LEAKEY'S - Church Street. Homely cafe serving soups, open sandwiches and salads etc within secondhand bookshop premises. Daily soup, inexpensive, flavoursome and nourishing. Tel: 01463 239947.

Shopping
The compact city centre means that nearly everything's within rushing back for your train distance of the station. High Street and Bridge Street are the main thoroughfares - the former being pedestrianised. Elsewhere, highlights are the VICTORIAN MARKET tucked away between the shop fronts on Academy Street, Union Street and Queensgate and readily visible from the Station Square. Its uncannily railway like architecture dates from 1891, the result of extensive rebuilding after a fire. Also on Union Street you might look out for THE GOURMET'S LAIR, a discrete little delicatessen offering some nice lines in local food and drink. Bookworms should make a bee line for LEAKEY'S on Church Street, reputedly Scotland's largest secondhand and antiquarian bookseller where there's usually quite a good selection of rail related titles. Tel: 01463 239947. More practically, there's a large SAFEWAY branch on Millburn Road just 3 minutes walk from the station.

Things to Do
TOURIST INFORMATION CENTRE - Castle Wynd. Tel: 01463 234353.
WALKING TOURS - guided tours of the city centre from the Tourist Information Centre on Castle Wynd. Tel: 07730 831069.
GUIDE FRIDAY - open top bus tours of Inverness, Culloden and Loch Ness. An excellent way to get a 'feel' for the vicinity. Tel: 01463 224000.
JACOBITE CRUISES - cruises on the Caledonian Canal throughout the summer from Tomnahurich Bridge, approx 1 mile from city centre. Tel: 01463 233999.
MORAY FIRTH CRUISES - short sea cruises from Inverness Harbour. Tel: 01463 717900.
MUSEUM & ART GALLERY - Castle Wynd. Local and highland heritage centre. Tel: 01463 237114.
CULLODEN MOOR VISITOR CENTRE - Culloden Moor. Approx 5 miles east of city centre; access for rail travellers by No. 12 bus or taxi. Tel: 01463 790607.
A 'Day Trips from Inverness' leaflet is produced annually describing numerous travel opportunities by train, bus and ferry to make the most of a stay in the locality. Contact the TIC on 01463 234353 or the ScotRail Travel Centre on 01463 239026 for further details.

Transport Connections
BUSES - Bus station adjacent to railway station. For all local transport information telephone the Highland Council helpline on 01463 702458.
CAR HIRE - Sharps Reliable Wrecks - Tel: 01463 236684. Office handily located on station concourse. Thrifty Car Rental, Harbour Road: 7 mins walk from station but if you pre-book they'll meet you off the train. Tel: 01463 224466.
TAXIS - Rank Radio Taxis - 111 Academy Street. Tel: 01463 221111.
CYCLE HIRE - Barneys - 35 Castle Street. Tel: 01463 232249. Open throughout the year 9am-9pm.

KINGUSSIE
Map 8

A 'fame thrust upon it' village, overcoming it's inbred rectitude in the spotlight glare of televison's immensely popular Monarch of the Glen series. Ideally located for exploration of the marshes and the mountains.

Accommodation
DUKE OF GORDON HOTEL - Newtonmore Road. Tel: 01540 661302. Another of those hotels which Queen Victoria stayed in. Newly refurbished. Three stars.
THE LAIRD'S BOTHY - High Street. Tel: 01540 661334. Bunkhouse accommodation.

Eating Out
ROYAL HOTEL - High Street. Tel: 01540 661898. Food and Iris Rose beers brewed 'out the back'.

Shopping
Post office, bank, chemist and food stores along the High Street, but on no account miss HAMLETT & GOW'S first rate butchers shop on King Street: award-winning haggis and home made pies!

Things to Do
HIGHLAND FOLK MUSEUM - Duke Street (5 minutes walk from station). Tel: 01540 661307. Open April to September. Hugely enjoyable interpretations of Highland life and history. Preserved buildings and farm machinery, craft demonstrations, historic furniture, country life and the farming year. See also under Newtonmore.
TOURIST INFORMATION - seasonal openings, housed in folk Museum foyer. Tel: 01540 661297.

RSPB INSH MARSHES - Tel 01540 661518. Beautiful floodplain and wetland environment. Hides and trails. Guided walks on Thursday afternoons April to August. Tel: 01540 661518.
RUTHVEN BARRACKS - spectacular ruin on high ground overlooking the Spey. A pleasant quarter of an hour's walk from the station.

Transport Connections
CYCLE HIRE - Service Sports, High Street. Tel: 01540 661228.

NEWTONMORE
Map 8

Rivalling Kingussie in its devotion to Shinty, Newtonmore can also claim to be the birthplace of pony-trekking, an activity still very prevalent in the area. Main Street is a peaceful thoroughfare since the A9 by-pass was built.

Accommodation
ALVEY HOUSE HOTEL - Golf Course Road. Tel: 01540 673260. Small three star hotel on the road to the golf course.
STRATHSPEY MOUNTAIN HOSTEL - Main Street. Tel: 01540 673360.

Eating Out
CAPERCAILLE - Main Street. Tel: 01540 673231. Scots-Italian restaurant which counts Chris Tarrant of *Who Wants to be a Millionaire* amongst its clientele.
THE PANTRY - Main Street. Tel: 01540 673783. Sweet little cafe for breakfasts, lunches and high teas.

Shopping
Post office, Co-op foodstore, craft shops and Bank of Scotland branch with auto-teller. All ten minutes walk from station.

Things to Do
HIGHLAND FOLK MUSEUM - Tel: 01540 661307. Twin centre museum (see also under Kingussie) devoted to celebrating and recreating traditional Highland ways of life. Voted 'Scottish Museum of the Year' in 2000. Fascinating for adults and children alike.
CLAN MACPHERSON MUSEUM - Main Street. Tel: 01540 673332. The clan system in general and the Macpherson Clan in particular.
WILDCAT TOURS - Main Street. Tel: 01540 673131. Information centre for Wildcat Trail and other local attractions.
WALTZING WATERS - Main Street. Tel: 01540 673752. 'The world's most elaborate indoor water, light and music production'.

High Street, Perth

PERTH
Map 1

A mysterious city of vennels and rows, so don't be put off by the dour approach on foot from the station. Persevere and Perth will begin to weave its spell; an attraction part historic, part atmospheric. The best approach for strangers is to acquire an 'Old Perth Trail' leaflet - obtainable from the Tourist Information Centre - which provides directions for two linked walks, an ideal introduction to its most characterful thoroughfares and buildings.

Accommodation
QUALITY HOTEL - Leonard Street (adjoining station). Tel: 01738 624141. The former Station Hotel now providing inexpensive yet comfortable accommodation.
RAMADA JARVIS HOTEL - West Mill Street. Tel: 01738 628281. Atmospheric water mill conversion from hotel group with growing reputation.
YOUTH HOSTEL - Glasgow Road. Tel: 01738 623658.

Eating Out
LET'S EAT - Kinnoul Street. Superb award winning restaurant. Not open Sundays or Mondays. Tel:

01738 643377.
LET'S EAT AGAIN - George Street. Slightly more relaxed offshoot of above. Highly recommended. Tel: 01738 633771.
KERACHERS - Scott Street. Tel: 01738 449777. Seafood restaurant.
OLD SHIP INN - Skinnergate. Tel: 01738 624929. Unspoilt traditional pub. Lunches. No piped musak!

Shopping
'Perth city centre has the best range of speciality shops in Scotland' to quote the tourist propaganda, and who are we to argue?

Things to Do
TOURIST INFORMATION CENTRE - Lower City Mills. Tel: 01738 450600.
SCONE PALACE - Tel: 01738 552300. 2 miles north of the city centre. 'An unforgettable day out'.
PERTHSHIRE VISITOR CENTRE - Tel: 01738 787696. Featuring the 'Macbeth Experience'. Located at Bankfoot (10 miles north of the city) which has had no passenger train service since 1931. Luckily there are buses!
HUNTINGTOWER CASTLE - Tel: 01738 627231. 2 miles north-west of city centre. 15th/16th century castellated house and ancestral home of the Ruthvens Connections with the Gowrie conspiracy of 1600.
PERTH MART - Tel: 01738 474170. Highland farmlife shows and retail outlets.

Transport Connections
BUSES - useful links along railway corridor to villages like Luncarty, Stanley, Ballinluig and Killiecrankie no longer served by train. Tel: 0870 608 2 608.
TAXIS - Perth Station Taxis. Tel: 01738 623400.
CAR HIRE - Thrifty Car Rental, St Andrews Street. Tel: 01738 633677.

PITLOCHRY
Map 4

Just about the perfect small Scots inland resort, though occasionally a tad too 'touristy' for its own peace of mind.

Accommodation
FISHERS HOTEL - Atholl Road (adjacent railway station) Tel: 01796 472000. Traditional three star hotel which thrived with the coming of the railway.
ATHOLL PALACE - Atholl Road. Tel: 01796 472400. Massive hilltop hotel in Scots baronial style. Not as expensive to stay in as you might suppose.
YOUTH HOSTEL - Knockard Road. Tel: 01796 472308.

Eating Out
CAFE BIBA - Atholl Road. Tel: 01796 473294. Well appointed modern cafe/restaurant, pancakes a speciality.
PORTNACRAIG INN - Tel: 01796 472777. Convivial riverside inn highly regarded for its bar food. Accommodation too.
THE OLD MILL - Mill Lane. Tel: 01796 474020. Bar and restaurant meals.
FESTIVAL RESTAURANT - Festival Theatre. Tel: 01796 484626. Excellent coffee bar and restaurant open throughout the summer season reached via a nice walk across the river.
PRINCE OF INDIA - Station Road. Tel: 01796 472275. Tandoori.

Shopping
All the to be expected craft, souvenir and gift shops, but some real gems as well, such as MACDONALDS BROS butchers on Bonnethill Road, MCPHERSONS fishmongery and greengrocery in Brook Place, MITCHELLS shop on Atholl Road for the fishing fraternity, and MACNAUGHTONS classic tartan and tweed shop on Station Road.

Things to Do
TOURIST INFORMATION - Atholl Road. Tel: 01796 472215.
FESTIVAL THEATRE - Port na Craig Road. Tel: 01796 484626. Summer theatre since 1951.
BLAIR ATHOL DISTILLERY - Perth Road. Tel: 01796 482003. Visitor Centre and tours of distillery which makes Bell's eight year old malt.
HEATHERGEMS - Atholl Road. Tel: 01796 473863. Factory shop and visitor centre devoted to jewellery and giftware.
PITLOCHRY DAM - Port na Craig Road. Tel: 01796 473152. Scottish & Southern Electricty visitor centre which interprets hydro-electricty and salmon. Salmon ladder and viewing chamber.
THE BOATING STATION - boat hire on Loch Faskally. Tel: 01796 472919.
CHILDREN'S AMUSEMENT PARK - Armoury Road. Tel: 01796 472876. Open Easter to October.

Transport Connections
CAR HIRE - HPTS, West Moulin Road. Tel: 01796 473066.
TAXIS - Elizabeth Yule, Station Road. Tel: 01796 472290.
CYCLE HIRE - Escape Route, West Moulin Road. Tel: 01796 473859.
BUSES - local connections to the likes of Killiecrankie and Rannoch (for the West Highland line). Tel: 0870 608 2 608.

INFORMATION

USING THIS GUIDE

Fourteen, north facing, one inch to one mile maps portray the route of the Highland Main Line between Perth and Inverness, including the Strathspey Railway between Aviemore and Broomhill. Each map is accompanied by a running commentary on matters historical, topographical and related to railway operation. Emphasis is given to the northward journey in each case, but the details are equally relevant for travel in the opposite direction.

Towards the rear of the guide a gazetteer gives details of all the stations on the route. This gazetteer gives a brief summary of each place together with itemised information on places to eat and find accommodation, shopping facilities, visitor centres, things to do and useful contacts such as bus links, taxi services and tourist information centres. Where accuracy is essential to the planning of an itinerary you are urged to make contact by telephone to ensure you have up to the minute details.

SCHEDULED SERVICES

Day to day services on the Highland Main Line are operated by ScotRail. Currently there are eight trains a day in each direction between Perth and Inverness; three of these originate in Glasgow, and five in Edinburgh. Additionally, GNER operate the *Highland Chieftain* through service to and from London Kings Cross. The average journey time between Perth and Inverness is two and a quarter hours. Services are currently provided by comfortable Class 170 Turbostar and 158 diesel units which provide both first and standard class, non-smoking facilities. Well stocked catering trolley services are available on the majority of services. A limited number of bicycles can be carried on ScotRail services - see opposite.

SLEEPER TRAINS

The Caledonian Sleeper runs nightly (Saturday excepted) between London Euston and Inverness via Edinburgh (and vice versa) and calls at all the Highland stations en route except Carrbridge. Very comfortable single and twin berth sleeper cabins are obtainable as well as a certain amount of ordinary seating between London and Inverness. A Lounge Car accompanies each train offering meals, snacks and drinks. **Telephone 08457 550033 for further details.**

CHARTER TRAINS

A number of companies run charter trains and excursions over the Highland Main Line. Often these will originate from other parts of the country and offer little or no opportunity for local travel.
Regular operators of excursions include:
SRPS Railtours - Tel: 01698 263814 www.srps.org.uk
The Royal Scotsman - Tel: 0131 555 1344
www.royalscotsman.com
Highland Railway Heritage - Tel: 01397 722295
Pathfinder Tours - Tel: 01453 835414
www.toursatpathfinder.co.uk
Hertfordshire Rail Tours - Tel: 01438 812125
www.traintrips.co.uk

TICKETS & TRAVELPASSES

There are ScotRail booking offices at Perth, Pitlochry, Kingussie, Aviemore and Inverness. A range of tickets is available from these offices and from the guards on board the trains. 50% discounts are available to holders of Highland Railcards. For an idea of fares (including current offers, Travelpasses etc) telephone **National Rail Enquiries on 08457 484950** or visit **ScotRail's website at www.scotrail.co.uk**
Tickets in advance are also obtainable from **ScotRail Telesales & Bookings. Tel: 08457 550033.**

HOLIDAYS

Fully inclusive Short Breaks, Self-Catering and Escorted Holidays featuring the Highland Main Line are organised by ScotRail - Tel: 0870 161 0 161.

BICYCLES

Bicycles are conveyed free of charge on ScotRail service trains. The diesel units which provide most of the timetabled services over the Highland Main Line can convey up to six bicycles per two car unit. Reservations are *compulsory* and should be made at principal staffed stations or ScotRail Telesales on 08457 550033 up to eight weeks in advance (12 weeks for the Caledonian sleeper service) but no later than two hours before the train *commences* its journey.

READING

The Highland Main Line by Neil T. Sinclair ISBN 0 906899 96 6
The Highland Railway by H.A.Vallance ISBN 1 899863 07 9
Railway Holiday in Scotland by Michael Pearson
ISBN 0 907864 90 2

VIEWING

Highland Main Line - Video 125 (Tel: 01344 628565)

USEFUL CONTACTS

HIGHLAND RAIL PARTNERSHIP - Lairg Station, Sutherland IV27 4EX Tel: 01549 402896. Email railzzz@btinternet.com
BRITRAIL - rail travel in Britain exclusively for overseas visitors. Very affordable and flexible rail travel options such as the **BritRail** and **Freedom of Scotland** Travel Passes. Visit: www.BritRail.net or call toll-free 1-877-677-1066 in USA and Canada.
PERTHSHIRE TOURIST BOARD, Lower City Mills, Perth PH1 5QP Tel: 01738 450600. Website: www.perthshire.co.uk
HIGHLANDS OF SCOTLAND TOURIST BOARD, Strathpeffer, Ross-shire IV14 9HA. Tel: 01997 421160. Website: www.highlandfreedom.com
NATIONAL RAIL ENQUIRIES - Tel: 08457 484950.

ACKNOWLEDGEMENTS

Wayzgoose extend grateful appreciation to the following individuals and bodies: Frank Roach and Alison Cavender of the Highland Rail Partnership; John Yellowlees and Alan Dougall of ScotRail; John Allison of the Highland Council; Dorothy Fenwick and Evelyn Brown of Railtrack Scotland; Doug Scott of the Strathspey Railway; James Shuttleworth of the West Coast Railway Company; Nancy Foy of Atholl Browse; David Alison of Tracks North; Hamish McEvison of the Friends of Riccarton Junction; Peter J. Robinson of Tynemouth and Jimmy Brown of Inverurie.

UNCAPTIONED PHOTOGRAPHS

Front cover: Culloden (or Nairn) Viaduct.
Back cover: The Royal Scotsman at Crubenmore.
Title page: GNER's Highland Chieftain at Slochd.